The Phantom Killer and Her Autistic Son

A Mother's Journey to Love and Acceptance

Grace Venters

The Phantom Killer and Her Autistic Son

Copyright © 2020 Grace Venters

Dedicated to my dear sons, William and Roderick,
and to all parents who share the same life-journey.

"One of the finest accounts of the experiences of a mother and her autistic son that travel together during forty years throughout a life marked by uncertainties, suffering, and also a good deal of joy.

The vastly unknown world of Autism is unveiled to the reader who joins Gracie`s passionate journey in her discovery of "Otherness". We cannot but learn and empathise with her each step of the way.

Not deprived of humour, this book shows the honesty and courage of a woman who makes the most of life while struggling to overcome distressful situations.

The Phantom Killer, written in a simple but engaging style, deeply moves the reader who is captivated by the singular relationship built by Gracie and her son.

Un-put-down-able!"

- Julie Mariano

"This is a beautiful book written by an incredibly devoted mother about her incredibly interesting autistic son! I really enjoyed reading it, learning more about William, laughing and crying with you. It was difficult to put it down until I finished it."

- Alba Steiner

About the Author

Grace Venters was born in Argentina, then lived for a year with relatives in Alabama, USA, before moving to the UK in 1978. Since then she has lived a few years in the UK, and a few years in Argentina, moving between countries several times. She is now settled in Hampshire, UK.

This is Grace's first book, and she has poured her heart out, letting her feelings and emotions come out from very deep within her.

This was written mostly for parents of autistic children, knowing that they would understand her life-journey, but essentially with the aim of helping them cope with their own life-journey.

This is a true story. Names have been used with permission.

Grace would appreciate your feedback. You can contact her on her Instagram page: @ventersgrace

Prologue

"I'm not weird, my brain is wired differently!"

Autism is a lifelong disability which affects how people communicate and interact with the world. *Lifelong* is the word that best expresses our joint adventure! It started when William was born and will be there for the rest of his life. William is different, and he sees the world from his perspective.

The title is based on some of William's stories, but you will have to keep on reading to find out why.

I hope *The Phantom Killer and Her Autistic Son* helps other parents of children with autism. Although each child is different, and their autism manifests itself in individual ways, many share the same traits and behaviours.

My journey with William has been like a rollercoaster, laughing out loud on the way up, and screaming on the way down.

I hope you enjoy my story.

Acknowledgments

I've wanted writing this book for a long time, but I really owe it to the persistence and encouragement of my lifelong friend, Ignacio Marcial Candioti who through the years pushed me to make a start! I had actually started it a few years ago, written a few pages, and left it. Last year I attended a lecture about writing and publishing given by a local author, Alice May, and I made up my mind to finish my book. The corona virus lockdown gave me the time and incentive to continue. Once I began writing I was unstoppable. Some emotions and feelings, that I was not even aware of, poured out and I had to keep on writing.

I'm truly grateful it to my dear husband, Nigel, who not only encouraged me, put up with my "please, don't even speak to me while I'm writing", but also gave me all the support I needed to keep on writing.

I would also like to thank my lifelong dear friend Julie Mariano, who from her own professional perspective made some helpful observations.

I'm extremely grateful to another lifelong dear friend, Alba Steiner, who with endless patience corrected a few mistakes (English is not my first language).

Last, but not least, I'm very grateful to Matt Watts, our son in law, who proofread my manuscript.

Chapter One

Saline, Fife, Scotland

William and I, June 2020

Has my "lifetime backpack" been any heavier than anybody else's? I don't think so! The difference is that mine has been designed to be carried permanently. Sometimes the load gets heavier. Other times it seems lighter. But the weight is always there, as if it is embedded within me. I "clean" my backpack every day to keep my mind sane and healthy. I throw over my shoulder what hurts me, in that way I can keep my load lighter. You need to keep it real, it's called happiness and success! Come with me through my life-journey, you will laugh, cry, and learn how I keep positive through difficult times.

My family is from Cordoba, Argentina. A big extended family with British roots. My parents had two daughters, my older sister (Dora) and myself.

In 1972, my sister went to Edinburgh to spend a year as an au pair. She attended some meetings of the Spanish Club, and there she met Reginald Elliott, who was trying to learn Spanish. Reggie was the owner of The Scotia Hotel, three Great King St, Edinburgh. Reggie and Dora became good friends. When my sister went back to Argentina, she told me everything about Reggie and his hotel. I was doing my last year of a degree in Tourism and Hotel Keeping. Having lived for a year in Huntsville, Alabama, USA, I was anxious to go and live abroad again. Argentina was going through a bad political period, with a military dictatorship, and lots of young people disappeared never to be seen again. So, I wrote to Reggie to see if I could come to work at The Scotia Hotel. As my grandmother was Scottish, from St. Andrews (Auchterlonie), coming to Scotland was a dream come true, and having a job in a hotel in Edinburgh was the cherry on the icing. Reggie and I became pen-pals (no internet then), started to write regularly and, strangely, we fell in love by correspondence. By this time, we were chatting through telex, and on the phone.

I graduated in December 1977, and left for Edinburgh. I was 23 years old. The hotel was not far from Princes St, the main street in Edinburgh. It had thirty-nine rooms, but very few had private bathrooms, as it was the norm in those days. The hotel was very popular due to its location. The restaurant also worked quite well and was full most days.

There were two permanent residents in the hotel, both of them quite elderly. One of them passed away not long after I arrived. And there is a funny story to it. This lady used to read the newspaper every morning, and her favourite section was the horoscope. On the day she passed away, her horoscope said: "You are going to go on a long journey"! The other lady, Mrs Ferguson, liked knitting, and she used to knit and pull apart, the same dishcloth over and over. She had curvature of the spine and used to hold her chin up with her hand. She was very chatty and cheerful.

In addition to the thirty-nine guest rooms, there were a few rooms for the staff, and I lived there for a month.

Reggie and I clicked as soon as we met. We felt like we knew each other quite well from our correspondence. Reggie was 23 years older than I. A very intelligent and interesting fellow, with many hobbies and abilities. Reggie was a fascinating man. He had a deep interest in wildlife, he bred butterflies, was a keen photographer, and developed his photographs in a dark room at the back of the house. He played the piano, spoke many languages, and was a member of the Tory party taking part in local politics. Reggie had a tremendous memory in general, but he had a specific ability to remember odd things, like the page and volume of the Encyclopaedia Britannica for information like battles or historical facts.

Reggie had been married twice before, but his previous wives were not able to have children.

A month after my arrival I moved in with Reggie. He had a lovely house in Saline, a small village near Dunfermline, in Fife. Reggie had bought this house in 1974 and had renovated it but without changing the character of the house, which dated from 1828. The house was called Burnbank. It was at the end of the village, with a "burn" at the bottom of the garden. There was an orchard and a vegetable garden. There was a small summer house in the lower garden where Reggie used to breed Black Veined White butterflies. He was trying to reintroduce them as they have become extinct. There was a small wood of Hawthorn trees at the bottom of the garden, and this is the food plant of these butterflies. As soon as they hatched, they were released onto the hawthorns, paired and they started to lay eggs on the trees, then we would collect the eggs and another life cycle started. I was soon hooked on this activity and we had endless fun collecting eggs and breeding. At the back of the house, there was a lawn with three slopes. There was a pond on the second slope, and some lovely Rhododendron bushes at the bottom.

Me in front of Burnbank

11

The views of Saline Hill and the fields beyond the house were magnificent. Burnbank was at the end of a gravel drive, and there was a cottage at the entrance of the drive, Drumhead cottage. The Rutherford family lived there. Bill and Peggy, with their teenage children: Penny, Stuart, and Alison. We became very good friends and shared many happy times. They helped me a lot to settle down in this completely new environment, and I am truly grateful to Peggy for all the help and support she gave me with the children, especially with William.

Life was good, we worked together in the hotel, had a lot of fun sharing different activities, travelling and meeting friends.

We were very sure of our feelings, and we both wanted to have children, so we didn't use any contraceptive methods and soon I was pregnant. We were both extremely happy. Reggie and I got married in July 1978.

My pregnancy was completely normal, I felt good and energetic. In my eighth month of pregnancy, the doctor was a bit worried as I had not gained enough weight, so I went into the hospital for a week, had lots of different tests but everything came out normal, and I went back home.

On the 11th of February,1979, at 13.00 hrs, William Henry Elliott was born by natural birth. He weighed 9.5 pounds and was 54cm long. Back in those days, first-time mothers were kept for 5 days in the maternity hospital to learn how to cope with a new-born baby. It was quite good as William was not an easy baby, he was hungry all the time. I did not have enough milk, so he didn't sleep long, and cried a lot.

And then it was time to go home with my dear baby. I was lucky to have Peggy to support me if needed. William would breast feed, then I would top it up with a bottle. This took a long time. Then I'd change his nappy and two hours later the routine would start again. He would not sleep in between feeds, so I was exhausted all the time.

Peggy would sing to William and rock him trying to get him to sleep, but as soon as one stopped, he would cry again. William didn't follow into a pattern of day and night as most babies do by the time they are around two months old.

William was growing into a beautiful baby, and, despite the sleepless nights, we were very happy parents. When William smiled, we would forget all the difficulties. We got used to sleeping for no more than 5 hours during the night, and it was a blessing if William slept at all during the day. We tried to live a normal life, and we were both positive and happy to have him in our lives. Our GP was confident that everything was all right and it was just a case of being first-time parents, and William would soon get into a normal routine.

William with me and with his dad

14

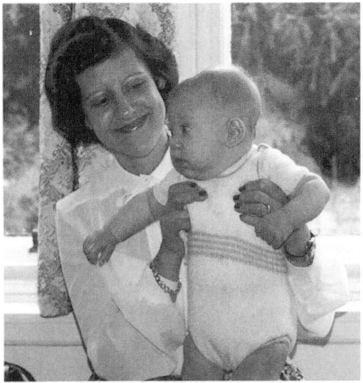

June, 79

In November 1979, we went to Argentina for 4 months. William was 9 months old. Cyril, Reggie's brother and business partner, stayed in charge of the hotel. We stayed in a summer house my parents owned in Unquillo, lower hills of the Province of Cordoba, which was surrounded by houses owned by close relatives.

My parents were waiting for us at the airport, eager to see their grandson, William, for the first time. My mother was a retired teacher of children with hearing impairments and special needs. When she saw William, she suspected there was something not quite right with him, but she didn't mention anything to me.

William went through his developmental stepping stones normally. He was sitting up by himself, crawling, walking, and all at the expected age. But his social behaviour was not normal. He was not trying to grab the spoon when I was feeding him, he was not waving goodbye, he was sometimes failing to look at somebody talking to him, and he was looking at my finger if I was pointing at something, instead of what I was pointing at.

He was not using his imagination when playing. He would turn a toy car upside down, make the wheels go round and round, and keep on at this activity for a very long time without losing interest.

On one occasion, William was sitting next to my cousin's daughter, who was the same age as him. She was paying attention to everything that was going on around her, and was participating socially, but William was in his own little world. But, so far, I had not started to worry, everybody was telling me that each child had their own unique development stages.

Soon after arriving in Argentina, we bought a second-hand car, a Renault 4, quite popular over there, and very suitable for dirt roads as it was a high vehicle. We removed the back seat and replaced it with a foldable cot. We went on a month-long trip to the Lake District in the south-west of Argentina. William travelled in his cot, happily entertaining himself, playing with his toys in his odd, but usual way.

Every night, as he was a poor sleeper, we gave him a mild sedative prescribed by the doctor. Even so, William did not sleep well. We had dinner early, and slept while William slept, but were exhausted most of the time. Having sleepless nights for a long period of time made us irritable, but we tried to enjoy our trip as much as possible. William was not crying much any longer and was happy playing on his own.

When we returned to Unquillo, I started to notice the difference between William's behaviour, and that of my cousin's children. But I still did not worry too much. We were almost amused, thinking he was going to be as eccentric as his dad, Reggie.

William was crawling at tremendous speed, with his hands and feet on the ground, and his bum in the air without using his knees. He was also walking holding on to everything for support.

As we were not really worried, we decided to have another baby, and I was soon pregnant again, and very happy. And in hindsight, just as well we did, as if I had known William was autistic, I would have never considered having another child.

We went back home to Saline, Scotland at the end of February 1980. A week after arriving, I had to take William for his annual check-up. His physical development was normal: weight, sight, hearing, etc, but they would not give me the written report my friends were getting for their children. When I asked for the report, they would tell me they were trying to gather more information, or they would be very vague about their response. I think they just did not know what was wrong with William and they didn't want to commit themselves to a diagnosis.

William started walking on his own in March 1980, and he loved to walk around the house and in our big garden. He loved to crawl up the stairs and come down head-first as if it was a slide. I must say that the stairs, and the whole house, were covered in a thick carpet. He would be at this activity for long periods, laughing loudly as he slid down head-first.

Both boys coming downstairs head-first

Around this age, he developed a great skill with his hands. He loved spinning things, from tiny pennies, hair rollers, and whatever he could find. He had two round toy mirrors, one concave, and the other one convex. He would stand one on its side on the table and spin the other one while he was looking at the standing one. He also loved the sound the mirrors produced on the marble table. We thought this showed extreme talent and intelligence.

Spinning a mirror and a round toy

William was also spinning himself round and round without getting dizzy, and at the same time looking out of the corner of his eyes.

He would build tall towers with small cubes, putting one on top of the other so they would not fall. And then he would topple them over, chuckling happily at his cleverness! He did something similar with small plastic tubes, standing three on top of each other, then he would look through the tubes and make them fall. He would make a perfect line with his toy cars, or play with the wheels, making them go round and round, for hours on end. He loved to be tickled, to be chased, to sit on my knees and gallop as my knees were a horse, the rougher the better.

When he was a year and a half, William's obsessive behaviour increased. First it was an obsession with certain foods, only soup for several days, then it was cereal and only cereal for days on end. After a few days, I decided to cut the cereal box back, an inch a day, until there was nothing left of the packet. I was quite happy with myself for this success, but, of course, another phobia took its place, such as only orange juice and biscuits, and only that for breakfast, lunch and dinner. I applied the same technique again, making the bottle disappear little by little, and the biscuit packet as well. As one obsession finished, a new one took its place. Making the box, or packet, disappear did the trick every time.

He developed some other odd behaviours. If I'd bought him new shoes, he would not wear them for some time, and then only at certain times during the day, standing on tiptoe in the same spot but not moving. After a few days of this, he would then recognise the shoes as his and was happy to wear them all the time.

He was fascinated by lights and shadows. He would spend hours opening and closing the small garden gate, watching the shadows that the iron bars of the gate made on the paved path. William would walk along in the sunshine, watching his own shadow and waving at the same time. He would spend a long time laughing happily in front of the washing machine while it was spinning.

He loved to "play" the piano, and he checked the sounds of the black keys against the white keys. But one day he developed some kind of fear and would not go into the dining room where the piano was. He would stand at the dining room door and look at the piano, but would not go in. There was a grand piano in the darkroom, but he was not scared of it. He was also scared of the dishwasher when it was on, but he loved the washing machine.

It was baffling to watch his behaviour and even more when other kids came to play. Reggie laughed away his worries saying that he was a chip off the old block. I was not so sure, but our GP was not too concerned and suggested he would grow out of it once he started nursery school and watched other children play "normally".

Watching the washing machine spinning

Cutting William's nails, and taking him to the hairdresser was a very unpleasant experience, with William screaming the whole time.

William was not starting to speak at all, and he was not making himself understood by pointing, he would just get frustrated and cry. He could understand everything that was being said to him, but he was not communicating back.

When I took him for his health check-ups I was told that speaking to him in two different languages was confusing him to begin with, and that all kids developed speech in different ways. I guess at that stage no-one knew what was wrong with William.

My second pregnancy was fine, and I could feel my baby kicking inside me. I was sure it was going to be another boy! I kept telling William about the baby, and made him feel my tummy when the baby was moving, but I don't know how much he understood as he was 22 months old when Roderick was born.

As William continued with his disruptive sleeping pattern, and was full of energy during the day, we thought it would be a good idea to seek help. We thought it would be quite helpful for William to have somebody to look after him during the first few months after the new baby's arrival. We decided to invite my aunt Haydee to come and live with us for five months. Haydee was about to move from Argentina to the United States, where her grown-up children lived, and she was delighted to come and stay with us until her daughters could sort out a place for her in Florida. This turned out to be a good move as Haydee was a tremendous help, as well as good company. Haydee was 67, of a happy disposition, and willing to help with whatever was needed.

William loved Haydee right from the start, and she spent hours chasing him around the house. William would stand on the step leading to the kitchen, waiting for Haydee to follow him and say: "I'm going to catch this boy!", then he would go down the step and run along. This activity would go on and on at different times during the day.

When my friends came with their toddlers for a visit, William always went to another room and played on his own with his toys. He would not share with the other kids, ignoring them completely. It was as if nobody had come, William was in his own little world.

William would relate well to me, Haydee, his dad, or any other adult that was prepared to play his games. He loved our neighbours, Bill and Peggy Rutherford, and their children. William especially liked Stuart Rutherford, as he would throw him up in the air and then catch him, the rougher the better.

William loved it when I read him stories, turning the pages as the story developed. He liked to listen to music, from classical to modern music. He enjoyed sitting on the stool to "play" the piano.

He was still not talking or communicating at all at 18 months old.

He didn't like to sit on the potty. He knew exactly when he was going to do a poo as he would go behind the door to do it. We bought several different potties, colourful, with animal shapes, a musical one, but he didn't want to use them. We left him without nappies to see if we could catch him in "the act", but he would do nothing, holding on until we put his nappies back on, or would just go behind the door when he was not being watched. I then bought a book that claimed that, with that method, I could teach my child to become potty trained in three days. I followed it right to the dot, but I was not successful. It was back to his nappies for some time, to try again, but William would not oblige. He hated the potties and the toilet!

On December 11th, 1980, our son Roderick was born. He was the same weight and length as William, 9.5 pounds, and 54 cm. Big babies. As it was near Christmas, the nurses had decorated the room with bright ornaments. Reggie brought William to see his new brother, but William was not interested in us, he only had eyes for all those bright, colourful Christmas ornaments.

After 24 hours in the hospital, we were allowed home. Just as well Haydee was there to help us! I will always remain very grateful for her physical and moral support; it was a joy to have her with us. As with any new-born baby, Roderick demanded a lot of attention, breastfeeding, and nappy changing. He did not sleep for more than an hour or two between feeds, and William was not sleeping either, so I was completely exhausted.

Baby Roderick

I was still using sedatives to try to get William into some kind of routine. When it was finished, I would start fretting and go back to the village doctor with an unbelievable story that I had dropped the medicine bottle, or left it in a hotel room. I'm sure he never believed any of these stories, but he must have seen how exhausted I was and must have taken pity on me, as he, reluctantly, would give me some more. This was not a permanent solution, and William was too young to be on sedatives.

Playing with Haydee

In March 1981, when Roderick was three months old, my parents came for a visit. They went on a tour of Europe that finished in Paris. We left Roderick with Haydee and Reggie, and William and I drove to Paris to meet my parents. We spent three nights in Paris and it was very enjoyable. From Paris, we went to London for two nights. William behaved well. William loved to be in his pushchair, being pushed along and feeling the wind on his face. (William was two years old).

Paris: having our portraits sketched

We drove back home with my parents, and it was lovely to see Haydee and Roderick again. My parents were over the moon to meet their grandchild, and also to see our house and our village. It is easier, when somebody talks about their daily life, if you can visualise where the person lives.

After a few days, we went to Oban, in the West of Scotland, to a self-catering complex of cabins, with a pub at the bottom of the road. We spent a few days there and went sightseeing around the Western Highlands. We used to take turns to go to the pub, and somebody stayed with the kids, usually me, but I managed to go a few times, and enjoyed the live music and dancing. We had to give Roderick a bath in the kitchen sink, but he did not mind. After 5 days we went back home, and soon after it was time for Haydee to leave us for Florida.

Before going to Paris to meet my parents, Haydee and I had been working in the front garden. We had planted some bulbs and done a bit of tidying up. When she left, she told me she had left a surprise for me. Haydee had a great sense of humour. Spring came and the bulbs we had planted started to grow, but along one of the walls, instead of irises, we had potato plants, and this was Haydee's surprise, she had replaced the irises with potatoes. We had a good laugh! Anyway, Haydee was missed!

My parents spent a month with us. My mother was worried about William, and so was I, but our GP and the Baby Clinic kept telling me that children develop in their own time. My mother loved children and she always developed a good rapport with them, but she was finding it difficult to relate to William. She told me that William was not keeping eye contact and looked "through" people. I had also noticed that and was very confused about his behaviour.

Finally, through my persistence, my GP said William might be autistic. I had never heard this word before, and thought he had said "artistic", haha. He also said that many kids presented this behaviour before they were 3 years old, but then they would grow out of it.

Dr Collins said he had no experience of autism, nobody had back then, but he referred us to a paediatric psychologist in Edinburgh. We went to this appointment, and the doctor thought that William did present some autistic behaviour, but he did not elaborate too much on what it meant, and he didn't seem to be overly worried about this diagnosis. We were about to go to Tenerife for 6 weeks. The specialist suggested that when we came back home, we would have a referral to go and see Dr Wholff, a well-known psychiatrist and specialist in autism. We hoped the long holiday by the sea would help William develop his language skills as we had more time to spend with both kids.

We went to Tenerife and stayed in a small cute flat in Playa de las Americas, which back then was a small fishing village. As William was still a poor sleeper, we used to go to bed and get up early. At 07:00 in the morning, we were already at the beach and would stay there until about 10:00 to avoid the strong sunshine. William loved the waves. I sat on the sand near the water with William on my lap and waited for the waves to cover us while he laughed happily. I tried it a few times with Roderick, who was a year old then, but he did not like it. William liked the sand, but refused to make castles, or anything productive with the sand. Our days were spent on the beach in the early morning, then a shower to get rid of the sand, and then we would go for a walk in the small town. Roderick was in his pushchair, and William walked. We would sit on a bench and watch William go up and down the many steps in the main square.

He just loved the stairs, and the steps going up and down to the flat.

Hit by a big wave/ Enjoying a walk at the seafront

And then our holiday was over, and it was time to go back home to Saline, Scotland.

◇◇◇

I had already concluded that William was not behaving normally. I went to the local library and borrowed all the books I found on autism; six books written by parents. As I started reading the first book, I could see that William shared the same antics as the kids in the books. After reading the six books I had already diagnosed William. He was obviously autistic.

Before going to our appointment with Dr Sula Wolff, I wrote a detailed report on William from when he was born up to that moment. Dr Wolff appreciated my report and diagnosed him as having autism. I must say that Dr Sula

Wolff was a very experienced child psychiatrist, and a lovely lady. I kept in contact with her for many years, and she gave me a lot of support and advice. It felt good to be able to talk to somebody who really understood what I was going through, who listened to me without judging me, and with whom I could discuss different suggestions on how to deal with different behaviours. Dr Wolff helped me to understand how the autistic mind worked. Although all children are different, certain behaviours are similar in all autistic kids.

William had his own "games" he wanted to play for hours on end. One of these consisted of him shaking his head vigorously until I said: "Don't do that or your head will fall off". He thought it was very funny and would keep on doing it for a long time. Another game he enjoyed was standing on the step, between the kitchen and the old scullery, and I had to say: "Jump down" and he would jump down, and then I had to say "well done." This was a source of much laughter!

He continued spinning round and round, without getting dizzy, and looking out of the corners of his eyes. He could keep this going for a long time, always smiling or laughing.

He loved spending time in the bathroom, taking out all the creams, sprays, etc., turning them over in his hands, and looking at them for a long time, watching how the creams or liquids run from one end to the other of the bottle. He would do the same with the detergent in the kitchen.

Another game was to go out to the lawn and look for some small dandelion flowers. William would place his foot just over the flower, but not stepping on it, said, "Mmm." Then I had to say, "Don't step on the flower", and this was very funny and he would chuckle happily!

In July 1981, William started to eat on his own with a spoon, a bit clumsily, but at least he was doing it by himself. William was two and a half years old.

The game, jumping from the step, changed to jumping from one pattern of the lounge carpet to another, but I had to keep saying: "jump over", he would jump, and I had to say: "well done", with a very emphatic tone of voice.

William liked kissing us on our feet, but never on our faces.

William loved playing with water. He has always been fascinated by it. There were two ponds in Burnbank, a small pond in the front garden, and a bigger one in the back garden. The front garden was walled, and William could stay there on his own, although we would either be outside, or watching him through the bay window. William would hit the water with the open palm of his hand and splashed. He loved doing this for hours. Sometimes we would provide him with a washing bowl full of water for him to splash in to his content.

Playing with water

William went through a period when he would grab Roderick from behind to make him fall backwards. I don't think he was jealous or aggressive, I think he saw it as a game. Roderick, who was still a bit unstable on his feet, was terrified of his brother.

William was not speaking, but he would love to bark like a dog. If we asked him what noise a dog made, he would bark three times, but if we asked him about a cow, a pig, or any other animal, he would still bark, but only once.

He was still ignoring the rest of the children, and would only interact with adults that were prepared to relate to him through his own games or antics.

The whole family

William enjoyed me reading to him, the same books over and over again. I taped them for him, and he would listen to the recording, turning the pages as the story developed.

Hearing tests (audiometry), and Eyesight tests were performed to see if he could hear and see properly. Since he was a baby, William has been able to hear through closed doors and walls. He has an incredible hearing which we had tested many times. We would say something, and he could hear it through the wall, even when we had talked in whispers.

His balance was also quite incredible. A test was performed in Edinburgh hospital to check his balance. I was asked to sit with him on my lap, on a rotating circular platform that started to spin. When it stopped, I was very dizzy and my balance had been affected, but William got down and started to walk as if nothing had affected him. Another test was standing inside a small square room that was slightly elevated and had no ceiling. The room floor would move backwards and forwards, and the normal body response is to keep your feet on the floor but follow the movement with your body, but William remained static.

We started with an assisted programme to help William. We went to a speech therapist, and to an educational psychologist, both in Edinburgh hospital. Sometimes, if the weather was good, we sat in the hospital grounds and had our sessions there. William started to say a few words, and he enjoyed these meetings. Now, at age 41, he still remembers going to the hospital for these sessions. I was grateful as, finally, something positive was being done and I had started to notice a little improvement in William's language. I think that the positive intervention, and a one-to-one approach of a professional definitely helped William. Although I was giving William a lot of my time, reading him stories and playing with him, I didn't have the same resources as this hospital department had.

They had more specific resources to teach children with special needs than me!

He was still refusing to use the toilet, and the psychologist suggested he could stay, for a few days in a special wing of the hospital which was designed to teach children toilet training. There were lots of stairs for William to go up and down, and he was happy to stay on his own. He didn't mind at all when we left him, which seemed odd to me but Reggie kept saying William was tough, chip off the old block, and I guess I wanted to believe this. He was there for three nights, and when we phoned to check progress, we were told that he was happy there but when they sat him on the toilet, three nurses had to hold him down and he would not perform. This might seem as a bit extreme, but I was following the advice of the psychologist and was desperate to get William toilet trained. The nurses said they had never encountered a problem like this, when a child refuses to actually sit on the toilet.

We came to the conclusion he was terrified of the toilet....and he came back home and to his nappies.

William started to go to the local nursery school in September 1982. His first day meant a lot to me as I had great hopes of "leaped" improvement. I had talked to him about being a big boy and starting school, and he didn't object at all being left there when I said goodbye. He seemed to enjoy going there, but he would not integrate at all with the other kids. William would spend most of the time jumping from one big cube to another, or would play on his own building cube towers, or turning the wheels of the toy cars. We were hoping that the interaction would help him, but there was no interaction, and the teacher could not spare any time to give him any one-to-one attention. Every day when I went to pick him up, all the other mothers were there, and William would hold on to any of the ladies, not looking at the faces to recognise his mother. This seemed very odd to me but Reggie kept saying he never recognised people unless he had met them several times, and he could not tell what people were wearing as he did not pay attention to these petty things....and probably William was the same.

For me, it was devastating to know that William was autistic, but Reggie would not accept it, and he thought that William was just lazy, that we were not strict enough with him, and that he had inherited his exotic ways. I did not have much support from Reggie, he kept saying that he was no good with little children, but that when they were both older, he would be able to talk politics, etc with them. It was difficult, as at that time, not a lot was known about autism, and the general public had never even heard about it. So, not a lot of sympathy from other people either. When William displayed odd behaviour in public, people would look at us and thought he was just being naughty.

I now believe that having a diagnosis for my son, and what all this meant, was going to be a long process of ups and downs, and that I had to go through it becoming stronger at every fall, more determined to cope, and incredibly resilient as I went along. At the beginning I felt very much alone, I did not have the support of my husband, the school, or even my village community. As time went on, I became stronger and learnt to find support from those who could understand me without passing judgement.

I have to mention here, that I come from a Methodist/Catholic family. My father's family were Protestants from different backgrounds, Methodists, Baptists, and an Argentine version of the Plymouth Brethrens. My mother was Catholic, but until we were teenagers, we all went to the Methodist church. My mother then told us we could choose what to do, but she was going back to the Catholic church. I shifted from one to the other, but mostly, remained a Methodist. When I went to live in Saline, there was a Presbyterian church in the village. My friend Peggy Rutherford, and most of the village, attended that church, and I decided it would be good for me to attend as well. It would also be an opportunity to make friends. William was baptised in this church on June 10th,1979 when he was four months old.

When William was diagnosed with autism, and I was heartbroken and feeling very low, none of the "elders" of the church came to see me. It was the duty of the Elders to visit people who were ill or distressed, but nobody from the church came to see me, neither the elders nor the other people I had met there.

I stopped going to church and was annoyed with God. Why on Earth, if William was loved so much, Reggie's firstborn after so many years of wanting a child, why did it have to happen to us? Why on Earth, so many bad mothers who had abandoned their children had "normal" children, and we couldn't? These are questions that have no answers,

43

and only with time, one starts to see things differently, and to accept the reality with a new approach. But I must say that, for Reggie, this was not so. Reggie could not accept that William was different. Reggie was not religious at all, and to him, this confirmed his belief that God was a man-made invention.

That following Christmas we went to Argentina for a month. William was 2 years and 8 months old. The difference in behaviour between William and my cousins' kids was very noticeable. That Christmas party, all the kids were involved in a manger, presents, Christmas songs, etc., while William was only interested in jumping from a slightly elevated porch during the whole party. We stayed in Unquillo, as we had previously done for the 4 months of our stay when William was 9 months old. As I said before, there were four houses in two acres of ground, with a low forested hill at the back of the houses. My uncle had put some steps going up this hill to a water tank. This was paradise for William, who would spend hours going up and down the hill.

Unquillo

When the sun was high in the sky, he would love to follow his shadow. One day we went to spend the day at an uncle's house near a big lake. There was a long stone wall around the garden, and William spent the day walking along the wall watching his shadow and waving at it. It was heartbreaking to watch the other kids playing together, and William playing on his own, ignoring everybody. My parents were devastated, especially my mother.

Following his shadow

We came back home to Scotland, and Reggie suggested that he wouldn't mind moving to Argentina, and he would like to breed butterflies to export to London Pupae Supplies, and that the rate of exchange would benefit us tremendously.

Reggie and Cyril (his brother) wanted to sell the hotel because there were new safety regulations, like fire doors, that would cost a lot of money to implement. It was sold quite quickly. In hindsight, it was not the best idea as it provided us with a steady income.

My parents suggested that it would be a good idea to move to Argentina as they could give us a hand with William.

I was in two minds about moving, on one hand, the idea was attractive as I felt I would have the support from my parents, relatives and friends, but on the other hand, I would lack the professional support that William was having from the Edinburgh team. In hindsight, I think we should have stayed put. It is always easy to say "if I had done this....", but nobody knows what would have happened if. I believe that if we had stayed in Saline,

William would have developed faster with the help of the professional team at Edinburgh hospital.

Chapter Two

Villa Silvina, province of Cordoba, Argentina

In August 1983, having sold our house in Scotland, we moved to Argentina. My parents had sold their house in Unquillo, but we stayed in one of the other houses that belonged to one of my aunts. We bought a small house in Villa Silvina, a small hamlet belonging to the parish of Salsipuedes, about 10 km from Unquillo. We were looking for a small house that we could renovate and enlarge to our own taste, and this house was just perfect. There was a big swimming pool, a BBQ thatched area, nice trees, and about two acres of ground. The place was on a hill and commanded great views. We just loved the place. The renovation was finished at the end of October, and we moved in. The children learnt to swim straight away, and we were happy to start our new life in this place. William seemed to cope extremely well with the move, from Scotland to Unquillo, and then to another house in Villa Silvina. William loves the sunshine, and he enjoyed being outside in the open air, swimming, and going for walks.

Our house in Villa Silvina

Not long after we had arrived, in August, I registered both boys at a nursery school in Rio Ceballos, a small town between Unquillo and Salsipuedes. William was three years and seven months old, and Roderick was two years and nine months old. From the first day, William was happy to go there, but Roderick cried a lot when I left him. Apparently, once I've disappeared, he stopped crying and was quite happy. This nursery school was situated in an elevated position behind the local church. There were some car tyres for the kids to play with, and William loved to roll them down the drive, and he would not tyre of this game, or from having to roll them up each time. He spent all his time doing this. Although it was good for him to attend this nursery school, he did not participate in many activities. William would look at books or sit in a corner while the other kids were singing and acting, but would not join in. Nevertheless, it was good for reinforcing his Spanish. Even if he did not participate, William took everything in.

On the other hand, Roderick enjoyed going to nursery and fully participated in all the activities. Both boys remained there until the end of 1983, and all of 1984.

Before going to Argentina, I had ordered, from the National Autistic Society, a lot of material to be able to teach William. I had flashcards with all sorts of subjects like activities, colours, sizes, etc. I also had a box with a Method to Teach Your Child How to Read. This was quite clever, and it used the shape of the words to teach how to read. William learnt quite a lot of words that he could then recognise in his books. I kept a record of William's progress on specific forms. I taught him shapes, sizes, adjectives, activities, and much more.

My parents lived in a very nice neighbourhood in the South of Cordoba city, about 45 km from our house, about an hour by car. My parents were very happy to have us nearby and came every Sunday to spend the day with us. Sometimes they would come and spend the weekend with us. My father was still working so they could only visit us on weekends.

As I mentioned before, my mother was a retired teacher of children with hearing loss and related problems, including autistic tendencies. In the same way that doctors are reluctant to perform surgeries on very close relatives, it is not easy to apply your professional knowledge to your own grandson. My mother was so distressed with William's behaviour that she could not help me in any way. Neither of them had a clue as to how to approach William. He needed, then and even now, for the other person to come down to his level, to his own games, and give the answers he wanted to hear. William wanted the other person to relate to him on his own terms. My parents never understood this and could not relate to their grandson. In a way, and I'm sad to say this, when my parents came to visit us, I was happy to see them, but it was hard work for me as they used to upset William. I think sometimes they took the hint and just ignored him. I'm sure William was happy to see them as long as they left him alone.

Life in Villa Silvina was good, and we were all happy there. We bought a miniature dachshund puppy and named her Pichi. The kids loved her. Roderick used to play with Pichi, but although William liked to see Roderick playing with her, he would not play with her or touch her. I had hoped Pichi might help him come out of his shell, but he was just happy to have the dog around on his own terms.

Jumping in the pool playing in the river

For Reggie to breed butterflies for export, we had a large metal frame, covered in mesh, built in the garden. The butterflies were mostly Papilio lycophron (later renamed as P. astyalus) and also P. thoas. The larvae of these butterflies feed on the leaves of a tree called Fagara coco (citrus family), and there were thousands of these trees in the area. At the beginning of the season, we would go searching for young larvae to start the breeding. William enjoyed these walks in the woods. In fact, we used to go for long walks around the area and William loved to join us.

At that time, Villa Silvina was a small hamlet of houses that belonged to different members of the same family, and as the older generation started to pass away, they sold the properties to non-family members. In the summer, the houses were occupied, but in the winter the families would only come at weekends. It was a very rural area, and we were very much on our own up there. This was Upper Villa Silvina, and there were more houses in Lower Villa Silvina.

One day, as we were walking down the road, we met a family that lived in Lower Villa Silvina, Mauricio and Pochi Guell, and their three daughters, Veronica (15 years old), Barbara (11) and Analia (9). We all became very good friends. They lived in the city of Cordoba, but would come to Villa Silvina every weekend and summer. Barbara and Analia became very good friends with our boys. Although they were older, they used to have a lot of fun together. They both related extremely well to both boys, and William loved to be with them. Both girls played with William on his terms, and he laughed a lot when they were around. I do believe that they were of great help to William. I am very grateful to both girls, and the whole Guell family, for all the support they gave me during those years in that area, and later on in life.

William had started to talk a bit more fluently, and I think all these games with Roderick and the girls helped him to improve his communication. Most of these games were rough and tumble games, chasing each other, running around, playing with the ball, jumping into the swimming pool, diving and looking for objects in the pool, playing in the river, throwing water at each other, and climbing trees.

Despite having perfect control of his bowels, he continued soiling his clothes. I tried several different approaches, focusing on one at a time. For example, I ignored him and just changed his clothes. I told him off, made him touch his soiled pants, made him rinse the pants, but nothing worked and it kept happening.

His sleeping was not any better. I had to stay with him until he would fall asleep, which normally took about two hours. When I thought he was asleep, I would quietly get up from his bed, but sometimes he was not actually asleep, and he would be awake for a long time as he anticipated I was going to walk away. About four in the morning he would come to our bed, Reggie would move to his bed, and he might sleep with me for another two hours and that was it, the day had started.

A friend recommended a psychologist who was into psychoanalysis and claimed she'd had some success with autistic children and I decided to give it a try. At that time, William spent a lot of time playing with a ball. He would throw the ball up to the roof of the house, and then loved to watch it roll down. Sometimes he would catch it, and sometimes the ball would go down the garden with William running behind it and laughing. When the ball rolled down the roof, William would say: "Ah, back". When I told the psychologist about this, she said that what William was saying was: *All Black*, relating his ball game to the New Zealand Rugby team All Blacks. I had never heard such crap in my life! We were not a sporty family, and we never watched sports on TV. It was very unlikely that William could have ever heard of the All Blacks. We never went back to the psychologist. I guess at that stage I was prepared to try anything that could have helped William, but if this would have been suggested now, in 2020, with all the available knowledge of autism, I would have never given it a try.

Playing with the ball and with Roderick

In 1984, I took William to a neurologist, Dr Cordoba, an excellent specialist. Several scans and tests were done on William, but none showed anything in particular that could explain his behaviour.

I developed an interesting relationship with Dr Córdoba, and we exchanged a lot of information about autism. I was a member of the UK National Autistic Society, and I was able to get a lot of front-line information. Dr

Córdoba, and I, took part in a TV programme to explain and talk about autism. This condition was still not well-known in Argentina. During this TV program I suggested that it would be interesting to form an association of parents of children with autism. Some parents called me, and we had several meetings with the aim to form this association. There were many bureaucratic obstacles to register the association, and in the end, very selfishly, I left them to struggle on their own. I'm saying very selfishly because I felt I had too much on my plate anyway, and I had the support of the UK National Autistic Society. I also felt (in my bones) that, in the end, we were not going to stay in Argentina for much longer. But at least I gave them the initial encouragement to make a start.

We used to go horse-riding almost every Saturday. My friends, Nestor and Rita Pizarro had a riding school in Unquillo. For several generations Nestor's family had owned a huge mansion, called La Providencia. Time had taken its toll, but La Providencia was still imposing. Our friend Nestor has seven brothers and sisters, and all had small children. We used to go on a horse trek, for about two hours, then stopping for a BBQ or a picnic, the children would play for a while, and then we would ride back returning in the early evening. There were always plenty of different aged children, to chase William about, and go along with his tickling and jumping games. When the weather was warm, we would stop by a river, and the kids would swim and jump from rocks into the many pools. William loved this and he would jump in from tall rocks.

Roderick soon learnt how to ride, but William did not like to ride on his own, so most times he was sitting in front of myself or Nestor. When we just started our horse-riding experience, Nestor used to take both my kids with him on his horse, one in the front of him and the other behind him!

Reggie did not like to ride, so he would go by car to the meeting point and join the picnic. Most Saturdays, Nestor and Rita would come to our house for dinner. Reggie and Nestor would play chess, and Rita and I would just have a good chin wag! We also went to La Providencia for huge BBQ parties. La Providencia was one of those places where a big crowd met. I think this was also very good for both kids and contributed to William's language and social improvement.

William, aged 5, was too old to keep going to the nursery school. There wasn't a nearby school that was prepared to take him. He started attending a school in a small village not too far away from our home. This village had developed around a quarry, and the people were poor but helpful and genuine. It was a rural school, where classes were small and there were mixed age groups including children with learning difficulties. The teachers were trained to deal with these difficulties, but they could not understand the needs of an autistic child.

In front of the school, there was a low stone wall. William would lie on top of this wall, and make undulating movements to stimulate himself sexually, panting at the same time. He just wanted to do this and would rarely participate in any of the class activities. This "game" did not go down well with the rest of the parents that thought their kids might copy his odd behaviour.

After a few months, I was asked to stop taking William to this school. Although I could see this coming, it was another blow for me, and another change for William. He didn't seem at all disturbed with the idea of not attending this school any more. William continued this behaviour at home as well. I thought he was a bit young to stimulate himself sexually, but there you are, he was doing it! I guess the other parents thought this was "a little monster", too advanced sexually for his age. I think he enjoyed the physical stimulation without the sexual connotation. Nevertheless, it was not appropriate behaviour in public, and it was embarrassing too.

When he was doing this at home, I tried to distract him and get him to do some other activity, and explained to him that this was not appropriate. Eventually, as with everything, in time he stopped.

So, I looked around for another school, but there was nothing available that specialised in autism, or that could deal with an autistic child as some schools in the UK. Eventually, I found a private organisation, run by an educational psychologist, called Granja Crecer. Granja is a farm, and this school was based on a small farm, with some animals, and the learning was done in a flexible approach that would suit William very well. It was expensive, and far from home. To get there I had to go into Cordoba city, and from there another 20 km more. There was not too much point in taking William there each day and going back home. Before I went to live in Scotland in 1978, I had worked, while studying Tourism, in a travel agency. Through my dealings with different airlines, I had met the owner of Iberia Airline branch in Cordoba and had become good friends with him and his daughters. We had remained friends through the years. I decided to ask him for a part-time job, and I got it. This suited me well as I took William to Granja Crecer, went to Iberia, worked there until 4pm and then went to collect William. William was happy at this school and was participating in the activities. We would get home at about 6pm. William loved his new school and was happy to take the trip there every day. I believe this school was good for William. Both owners, Cristina and Alberto, were educational psychologists and worked with William on a one-to-one approach.

In June 1985, Reggie came to the UK to talk to his stockbroker, his bank, and to deal with a few other issues. He was here for the whole month. As well as taking William to his Granja Crecer, I had Roderick in nursery school. Fortunately, a family lived next to the school, and their young daughter (12 years old) used to help there. Roderick loved Carmela, and I asked her if she would babysit him in their home before and after school. Carmela was happy to do it, and it was the perfect solution for me. I took Roderick there, then William to Granja Crecer, went to Iberia, picked William up, then picked Roderick up, and got home about 6.30 pm. It was twilight then, and our house was quite isolated, but I was not scared and managed quite well on my own.

One story that William always remembers, and still talks about it now, in 2020, is when we went for a walk, just the two of us, and we had done about 500 yards when we heard the house alarm beeping loudly. I then remembered I had left a door open inside the house. We started running back, William's shoes came off, we had to stop to put them back on, and continued running until we reached the house and turned the alarm off. When he tells this story he always gets me to make the sound of the alarm!

William has always been fascinated by death, and if we were out walking, and we saw a dead animal, William wanted to stop to have a good look. One day, coming back from the supermarket, there was a bad car accident, the ambulance was there, and there was a body covered by a white sheet. William wanted to stop to look at the body and cried all the way home as I didn't want to stop.

Although this is 2020, the real cause of autism is still unknown. There are several theories about chromosomes, genetic mutations, metabolic imbalances, etc. I'm inclined to think that, in William's case, genetic inheritance could well be the cause. Most people, at the top of the autistic spectrum umbrella, could function fairly well in society, and even have a brilliant job. Some people are highly regarded professionals and are very intelligent. An example is Alan Turing, the person who devised the technique which cracked the German Enigma code during the Second World War. Most of these people had been considered eccentrics. Nowadays, "eccentric" people are being diagnosed, even at a late age. Some of these people, with Asperger, or mild autism, could even be in a relationship, although most times it is not a very successful one.

Reggie's father, Thomas Elliott, was English but living in Scotland, and took part in the first World War. He got married to a Russian Jewish, Fannya Bonnesky, whose family had escaped from Russia and relocated to

Edinburgh. Thomas had a hotel called Edinburgh Grosvenor Hotel, on Grosvenor St, Edinburgh. The family lived in the village of Balerno, 8 miles south-west of the city, in a very big mansion. They had maids, and a governess to look after Reggie and his brother Cyril. The children attended George Watson's Private School for Boys (now George Watson's college, co-educational independent day school), a very expensive and exclusive school. So, Thomas Elliott was the Lord of the Manor, and the owner of a prestigious hotel. Their house was at the edge of the village. On Sundays, Thomas rode his bike to the village shop to buy the newspaper…nothing unusual in that, but the weird thing was that he went in his pyjamas and house slippers! Strange behaviour for the Lord of the Manor!

When Thomas was at the hotel, working, sometimes a supplier, or

a colleague would come to see him. The receptionist would come to Thomas' office to let him know, and, if Thomas was not in the mood, he would just say: Tell him I don't want to see him. This is not socially appropriate. One would say: Tell him I'm very sorry, I'm awfully busy but I could see him tomorrow, or Tell him I'm not here, etc.

Thomas had a very big Bentley...this was probably in the late 1930s. One day he had parked the car in front of the hotel, and when he finished work, he got into his car and drove home. He could see in his mirror that a smaller car was following him rather too close for his liking. When he got home, he realised that the car was not following him. When he had started the car, after work, he had reversed it, hooked the car behind on his bumper, and "towed" it all the way home.

Thomas had some odd behaviours, was an introvert, but his wife made up for it as she was very outgoing.

Reggie also had some odd, and eccentric behaviour, topped up with an extraordinary memory.

When Roderick was going to Kindergarten, either Reggie or I drove him there. We had two Renault 4s, an older model, and a new one top of the range. This new one was red. One day, Reggie took Roderick to school, and when he got home, I could see that he was driving a red Renault 4, but it was not ours. How on Earth he had managed to use our keys on a different car, only God knows. This Renault four belonged to one of the teachers and had a child seat on the back seat. He had to drive back to the school, excused himself, and drove our car back.

◇◇◇

My sister and her family lived 5 hours away from Villa Silvina in the city of Santa Fe. My sister has three sons and a daughter, and Roderick got on very well with his cousins. Sometimes Roderick would go and spend a few days with his cousins in Sante Fe.

I must say that the support and love of my sister, my cousins, uncles and aunts, and all my friends, helped to keep me sane and happy during all the hard times with William. I believe that our time in Villa Silvina was very enjoyable and happy, maybe the happiest one in our marriage. We had a lot of difficult times with William, but very happy times as well.

William continued with his fixation with bottles. He loved turning bottles upside down to see how the liquid would run from one end to the other. If we went to visit friends, he would go to the kitchen and look for washing up liquid, bleach, or any other product. He could spend hours doing this. He never took the lids off, just turned them upside down.

Another of his antics was to get the bit at the end of a biro pen, the one that holds the ink tank in the pen, remove it and then put it back. We called it: the bit that goes inside. The main problem was that this bit was small, and sometimes it got lost, and then all hell would break loose. There was no point in giving him another bit from another biro, somehow, he knew it was not the correct one. We then proceeded to look under the furniture, between the cushions of the sofa, under the beds, everywhere, until the bloody bit appeared! This "game" lasted for a long time, and William could not resist a biro that he could not take apart!

In October 1986, we went to a self-catering complex of cabins in the small town of Villa General Belgrano, towards the south of the Province of Cordoba. Villa General Belgrano is a town that developed from the survivors of the Graf Spee, a German battleship that was scuttled by the Germans at the estuary of the River Plate, only three months into the WWII conflict to avoid possible sinking by the British Navy, which was waiting for the Graf Spee to go into the port of Montevideo for urgent repairs.

If anybody was dropped there by parachute, without knowing the location, he could not be blamed for thinking he/she had landed in a town in Germany.

We loved going to this area, and we visited this town many times during our stay in Argentina. We liked these cabins, owned by a German couple. The complex is still open, and it is called Berghutten. It is now owned by this couple's son. We had been there a few times and the kids enjoyed the huge park where the cabins were located, the swimming pool, and going into town to have an ice-cream or a meal.

As soon as we arrived, I told William that if he wanted the toilet, he should tell me as there was not a separate sink to wash soiled underwear. I told William to let me know if he needed the toilet all the time but he often ignored me.

In the afternoon, we were about to go into town to do some shopping, when William said: Poo, and I thought he had soiled his pants again, but he actually wanted to use the toilet. And that was it, from that day onwards he never soiled or wet his pants again. William is like that, once he decides to do something there is no looking back. William had, at age 6, simply decided that he was not going to wet or soil his clothes anymore, and that he was not scared of the toilet any longer. It felt great to know that we have overcome this and it was such a step forward. I was beginning to learn that William needed his own time to work out how to solve his own issues.

At the end of October 1986, the owners of Granja Crecer, a married couple, both educational psychologists, decided to split up, and that was the end of Granja Crecer. I became a bit upset at the lack of opportunities for William in Argentina. The economy of was in chaos again, and we made the decision to come back to the UK.

I was a member of the National Autistic Society, and they suggested that, according to my description of William's strengths and weaknesses, a school for autistic children near Tavistock could be well suited to his needs.

We were flying back home with Panam Airlines, via Miami. Our flight was on December 27th, from Buenos Aires to Miami, a wait of 12 hours, and then Miami to London. Reggie and the kids, having British passports, did not need an American visa, but I did as I had an Argentine passport. I phoned the American Embassy to make sure the embassy would be open on the 26th, and they confirmed it would be. We went to Buenos Aires on the 25th, stayed in a hotel, and on the 26th at 7am I was outside the embassy ready to get my visa. There was a sign on the door saying that they had decided to close the embassy that day as it fell on a Friday, between Christmas Day, and the Saturday. So, I did not have a visa, but we did not think this would be a problem as we were in transit. As we had a long wait in Miami, we intended to stay, for those 12 hours, at the Miami airport hotel. When we arrived at passport control, Reggie and the kids went through without any problem. The agent looked over the counter, gave me a filthy look, and told me: "You have stepped over the yellow line, you are now in the United States, and you are an illegal immigrant." I could not believe my ears! My passport was retained, and I was assigned a policewoman who stayed with me for the duration of my stay. She was really good and understanding, but her job was to stay outside the hotel room door, and then with me until I was safely in the airplane. An hour before we were due to board, we went to the airport lounge, but the flight was delayed. At some time, while waiting, Reggie went to the toilet. The gate opened for boarding, but we could not find Reggie. We asked a gentleman to check in the toilet, but Reggie was not there. I was getting anxious as they were calling for boarding. Finally, we found Reggie under a row of seats sound asleep! We boarded the plane and arrived in London! (William was almost 8 years old, and Roderick was 7). All in all, it was a very frustrating and stressing time, but William behaved quite well considering all the problems we had. William loved flying and this helped to make the change. I talked to him about coming back to Britain and he seemed quite happy. I was looking forward to getting the support I needed for myself and William.

We stayed for a couple of days in London and then went to Edinburgh for a few days. While in Edinburgh, we stayed at the Marriott Hotel. This was a new hotel, with a swimming pool, jacuzzi, and a gym. William was delighted to stay there, and he spent a great part of the day at the swimming complex. We bought a car while we were in Edinburgh, a Renault 21, which was then top of the range of the Renault models. This proved to be a mistake as it was too wide for the narrow lanes of the West Country. We also took advantage to visit Cyril and family, and some of our friends.

After a few days, it was time to go to Tavistock and start our new life there. So, we paid our bill, and collected the children. When William realised that we were checking out of the hotel, he absolutely refused to go out of the room. I had to hold his legs, and Reggie his arms, and dragged him out while he was screaming at the top of his lungs. It was a tragicomedy as the manager told us to wait while he was getting his video camera. He wanted to film this event for publicity, the guests did not want to leave and had to be dragged out of the hotel. Later on, William thought it was very funny, and so did we...but not at that moment when we had to drag him out while screaming. Even now William tells this story to anyone who cares to listen, and he laughs at the thought of him being dragged out. Now it is 2020, and we have been going to the Marriott every June for about 15 years. The first time we were back, after that famous stay, William noticed that the hotel carpets had been changed, they used to be blue at the end of 1986!

Chapter Three

Tavistock, Devon, England

We drove from Scotland to Devon, going across Dartmoor in the south-west. We arrived in Tavistock, and booked into the Bedford Hotel, for a couple of nights, to give us time to look for suitable self-catering accommodation. It was the middle of winter and very cold.

All the self-catering flats were suitable for the summer and warmer weather, but not for that extremely cold winter. Finally, we convinced the owners of a flat in Yelverton (5 miles from Tavistock) to let us rent it for a few weeks until we could buy a house. This flat was very nice, built over a four-car garage, with one bedroom, bathroom, a lounge and a kitchenette. As it was built for the warm weather, the windows were single glazed. January 1987 was the coldest winter for 100 years, with temperatures of -20C at night. We used to put newspapers on the windows to keep the cold out. We had an electric heater, but it was not enough to keep the flat warm. Just as our ancestors used to do, we just wore thicker clothes and even coats inside the flat.

There was a sofa bed in the lounge for the kids to share at night. It converted into a double bed, and they were happy to sleep together. Fortunately, this helped with William's sleeping problem, and he finally slept through the night. Hallelujah! One problem sorted! From then onwards, William decided to sleep through the night without me having to stay with him until he fell asleep or coming in the middle of the night to our bed! As usual, William made a decision, and there was no looking back! I was slowly learning that I could help William as much as I could, but in the end, it was his decision and he had to reach a milestone in his own time. My help, support, and social stories contribute to him making his decision. This applied then and now.

This sofa had an unusual system of converting into a double bed. It had a frame that held the seat cushions in, then there was a cover that covered the whole of the seats. (I am not sure what the purpose of this was). Then the back of the sofa went down, and the bed was made. The seats, within the frame, could be removed, and the cover pulled over the rectangular gap the cushions left. It might sound complicated, but the purpose of this long explanation is for you to understand that there was a rectangular hole, that could be covered by a thick cloth (the cover), and produced a kind of "den", "cavern", or, as Roderick called it: Their Hut! William has always loved small tight places, corners, dark cupboards, and tents. The Hut gave them endless hours of entertainment, staying inside with Roderick talking to William, getting in and out, and just happy to be hidden there for a long time. Sometimes Roderick will set it all up for William, but only William would get in while Roderick played with his toys.

We looked at many properties, and finally, we saw one that we both liked. As I have mentioned it before, we lived on the stock market, where the money from the hotel had been invested. Reggie was tired of working, but mostly of being an owner-manager where all the responsibility was on him. I was still young and eager to keep on working. There was a lovely guest house for sale, just outside Tavistock, on the road to William's school. It was at the top of a sloping garden, in a prime position. It had five guest rooms, apart from living quarters for the owners. This was a very manageable proposition and I would have loved to own it. William was at school most of the time, and, as it was a boarding school, William could have stayed overnight if I was too busy. Reggie would not have it; he did not want anything to do with any kind of business proposition. In hindsight, this could have saved our finances.

We bought a very nice house in town on a one-way street coming down, and we had to park the car at the top of the road. The house had three bedrooms, and a loft conversion. The loft room had a Velux window from which the whole of the town could be seen. It was a beautiful view and I was never tired of it. The kitchen had a lovely red Aga cooker that, apart from cooking, heated up the top floors, and produced all our hot water. I loved my Aga. There was a pantry off the kitchen. The house was full of character. Downstairs there was a medium-size lounge, separate dining room, a long, narrow conservatory, and a toilet. The toilet had the downpipe visible and painted in red. It had Laura Ashley wallpaper, and bookshelves on the wall. The kids shared a room, and we bought bunk beds with headboards that looked like cars. The third bedroom was used as a darkroom, music room (the piano was there), and library. The loft room was our guest room. There was a tiled patio at the front, a small garden outside the conservatory, and then it went down a path to a walled garden. This wall garden had been properly landscaped with bushes that flowered at different times of the year. We moved in in the middle of February, and it was a relief to have our own house, with our own furniture and things. Tavistock is a lovely town, with the river Tavy flowing through it, and a big park with a canal. It is a town built in different levels, which makes it very attractive.

Our house in Tavistock

As soon as we got settled in Yelverton, before buying our house, Roderick started going to Tavistock Primary School. He took a couple of weeks to settle in. Although his

English was very good, he spoke adult English, and he did not have the children's vocabulary, nor the slang words. But he was soon part of the group, and he loved his school. We used to go to the Assemblies, and Reggie recorded many of them with his video eight camera. Roderick worked through his school curriculum, and very soon caught up with the rest of the class. He got several swimming certificates, and he showed how bright he was. Reggie and I loved that school, and we could see how good it was for Roderick, and the stimulation and encouragement he got there.

One day we went to shop for Roderick's school uniform. It was very cold, it had been snowing and it had turned into ice, very slippery. Roderick and I hated it, but William loved it. As soon as we went into the shop, William spotted one of the Sales Assistants who was holding a pen to her mouth. He ran to her, grabbed the pen, took it apart, and the bit that goes inside was lost! Oh my God, what a situation! The Sales Assistant could not believe what this child had done, and at what speed. William had hurt her mouth when he grabbed the pen, and she thought he was just very naughty. In those days, when I explained that

William was autistic, it didn't mean much as people did not know about this condition. Anyway, to continue with the story, everybody in the shop was looking for the "bit that goes inside". People were looking under stools, amongst uniforms, inside school shoes, etc, and finally, William found it under a shelf. Of course, as usual, from screaming and very upset, he switched off and was happy again. I convinced him to give the pen back to the Sales Assistant before leaving the shop, with the promise of buying him his own pen with a bit that went inside. Everybody was happy, and most of all the Sales Assistants who had got rid of us!

Roderick in his school uniform

William started going to Gulworthy School for Autistic children, in Gunnislake, about 2 miles from Tavistock. This school was run by Mr and Mrs Mumford and was accredited by the National Autistic Society. There were only ten children in the school, one of them was a girl, two were twins, and William was the youngest. One of the boys had to wear a helmet as he used to bang his head against the wall. William loved his school, and he used to get up, and look forward to his day at Gulworthy. He went there from 9am to 4pm. Collin was his teacher, and he was excellent with William. William learnt how to do his buttons up, how to undress and dress again, his reading and writing improved considerably, and he developed many more independent skills. Once a week they took all the kids to a swimming pool in Liskeard, and another day they went to a gym. The gym had all sorts of equipment like climbing frames, narrow elevated boards to walk on for balance, and a huge ball pit that was William's delight. William loved to jump into this deep ball pit, and better still if Collin picked him up and threw him in. The school was surrounded by a very big garden, with some low apple trees, a swing and a slide. William enjoyed climbing the low trees, and the playground games.

William, front right, with some of the kids and teachers

We used to pick up Roderick, from school, and then went to pick up William. Between Tavistock and Gulworthy, there was a Harvest Inn pub, with a nice beer garden and a playground for the kids. There was a treehouse, in the playground, with a slide coming down from it. Both kids loved to go there, and they had endless fun going up to the tree house and down the slide. There were usually other children playing there, and William loved to be chased up the stairs to the tree house. Sometimes he just sat at the top of the slide for someone to push him down. We also enjoyed our time there, we could have some

81

peace while the kids played for hours, and then we all had a meal.

There was an indoor "diving pool" in Plymouth, with a 10-metre diving board. We took William there from time to time, and he jumped from the diving board without any fear!

It was a nice spring, and we went for many walks, picnics, going to the beach to pick up mussels and cook them there on an open fire. We used to go walking, with our wellies on, along a tidal river when the tide was down, it was muddy but fun. William was happy when we had an outdoor activity. We used to go to Looe, rent a power boat, and spend some time motoring around the bay. Sometimes Reggie sat Roderick on his knees and let him steer the boat! Polperro was also one of our favourite places to go. When the tide was out, we could walk along the beach and into the Smugglers' caves.

I was trying to teach William how to count. I was doing this to reinforce the work done at school. I had several copybooks and had stuck pictures on them. I had started this in Villa Silvina. I had a notebook for pictures of one item: One chair, one horse, etc. Notebook number 2, with pictures of two items, and so on. William enjoyed going through the notebooks and, if I asked him how many things, he would always get it right. Obviously, he had memorised them and he knew exactly how many items in each notebook. If I asked him, in real life, e.g., how many glasses on the table, or how many trousers on the bed, he would answer anything but the correct answer. I was growing a bit upset and thought he would never learn how to count. One day, we went for a picnic next to a field. There was a gate and a field with many cows. William stood on the gate and started to count the cows. I could not believe my ears! He knew how to count all along, but he could not see what the purpose of my questions were. If I knew how many glasses were on the table, or trousers on the bed, why ask him? From then on, he always counted things pointing with his finger.

Sometimes, Reggie and I were in the lounge, and William would be in the dining room writing in his notebook, and we would be discussing William and his problems. We soon realised that William could hear us between the walls, and he looked upset. He knew we had been discussing him. It made me very sad to think about his feelings and we were very careful in the future to talk about him when he was at school or not around.

◇◇◇

We went to London for a few days, and we took the kids to Trafalgar Square. Back then, there were thousands of pigeons in Trafalgar Square, and one could buy seeds to feed them. This was like his dream come true. He put a lot of seeds on his head, and the pigeons made a beeline for it, landing on his head and picking at the seeds! What fun! I must have bought about ten containers with seeds...most went on William's head, but no bird took him flying! Roderick was more sensible and liked throwing the seeds on the floor for the pigeons to gather there.

William continued to make progress at school, learning to read and write properly, and improving his independent skills. The school had lent us a big tricycle for William, but he was not very interested in it. Roderick tried to teach him how to ride but, most of the time, Roderick or I would ride it with William standing at the back holding on to us. As long as somebody else was riding it, William loved going on it. We used to take the tricycle down to the park and go riding for a long time. Sometimes we stopped and fed the many ducks on the canal. Both kids loved to feed the ducks.

Reggie, William and Roderick on the front patio

While the kids were at school, I decided to make cakes and sell them at the Women's Institute stand at the weekly Pannier Market. As our Aga cooker was on all the time, I would only spend money on the ingredients. Part of the profit was for me and the rest for the W.I. It was fun and I made some friends.

There was a big covered market building, and there was a different market every day. One day it was dedicated to swapping things, and I used to swap the children's toys. It was quite good as the kids got "new" toys every so often. Most of the toys were Fisher-Price, or similar, so they were good quality toys in good condition. I got William a Fisher-Price record player with five records, of different colours playing Nursery Rhymes. William loved his record player and spent hours playing his songs. One day we were all in the lounge, Reggie reading the newspaper, William with his records, and Roderick reading aloud some book he needed to study for a lesson. Roderick got frustrated as the Nursery Rhymes songs were interfering with his reading...and he had started reading before William had come in with his records. Roderick asked his brother to move to another room, William hit Roderick's book with a record, and Roderick told him he was an effing fucker! Obviously, Roderick had learnt some colourful vocabulary at school pretty quickly! (William loves telling this story).

I had met some of the kids' mothers at Roderick's school, and had made some friends, especially with an Australian family. Our two families used to meet quite frequently, and many times either Roderick went to sleep over there, or Andrew (their son) would come to our house.

My uncle and aunt, Edwin and Betty, came to visit us in the summer. It was good for both kids to have relatives staying with us, and we took the chance to travel around quite a lot. Edwin and Betty were very patient with William, and he enjoyed having them around.

Roderick was obsessed with Superman at this time, wanting to wear the costume during the day, and sitting on the bottom step singing the Superman song and tapping his feet on the floor. William could not understand what was going on with his brother.

That summer we got a biggish paddling pool, and the kids had a lot of fun splashing around when the weather was good.

We went for a holiday to Gwithian Sands, near St. Ives, in Cornwall. We booked into the Gwithian Sands Hotel, and there was not much more around there. We could walk to the village pub, and the beach was just on the doorstep. Gwithian Sands is famous for the sand dunes. The hotel had a small indoors swimming pool, and, obviously, William was hooked. He liked to go to the beach as well, and play with the waves, but mostly, he wanted to stay in the pool.

One day we decided to go and visit St. Michael's Mount, which is a replica of the original in France. It can only be accessed by a causeway that is exposed when the tide goes out. William didn't want to go, but we went anyway. The causeway is quite long, and it takes about 10 minutes to get through. The paths around the castle are cobbled and steep, and it takes about two hours to visit without spending much time exploring. The whole time, after getting out of the car, William held my hand and continually repeating, 'Don't want St. Michael's Mount'. It was like a chant! But we were determined, for our sake, and for Roderick's sake, that we were going to take advantage of the holiday to visit all these places. Reggie, of course, recorded these antics with his video camera, much to my annoyance!

The school year started, and I had some time in my hands. I wanted to do some work, something more stimulating than making cakes for the market once a week. I got a part-time job, three times a week, as a teacher's aide at Mount Kelly's school, and I also volunteered at

Roderick's school to teach cooking. I thoroughly enjoyed both jobs.

William grew out of his biro fixation (the bit that goes inside), and music became the new obsession. We had a big collection of Vinyl records, and cassettes, and he learnt how to operate the HiFi.

When the cold weather started, Reggie was happy to sit by the stove, powered by anthracite, to read his daily newspapers. I must say that the weather in the West Country is not the best. Tavistock receives a lot of rain. The humid air from the Atlantic hits Dartmoor and falls in Tavistock. The old adage that the rain falls in the plane, at least in Spain, is not true, all the rain falls in Tavistock! But, when the sun came out, it couldn't be more beautiful. I loved Dartmoor, and we went there many times for walks or just a drive. Reggie was still involved with the kids, attending Roderick's school assembly, going with me to pick up William, and for walks when the weather was good. He was still taking some photographs and developing them but had more fun with the video camera.

Sometime during the autumn, my dear friends, Alba and Denis, went to spend some days in a National Trust cottage in Bovey Tracey, at the edge of Dartmoor. We all went to visit them. Alba had made a chocolate cake and had put it on a coffee table. William picked up the whole cake and started eating it! Fortunately, it was just a sponge and it didn't have any icing! We all had a good laugh!

I was reinforcing the concepts that William was taught at school. We were playing matching games, getting to make phrases like: a tube of toothpaste, a tin of beans, a pair of shoes, etc. We also gave him complicated instructions like: bring me the book that is in the dining room, under the newspaper that is on the table. William liked these games and did well! The school had provided us with teaching material as well as with forms to record William's progress. All this was very encouraging and I could see William progressing, and most important, he was happy.

William's teacher taught him how to tell the time and he really enjoyed what he called "Time games": I would tell him the wrong time for him to correct me, or viceversa.

William loved to see the different clocks on church towers, or in buildings. Big Ben was his favourite! Wherever we went he would be looking for the church to see if there was a clock. He became obsessed with time, and he would be asking me what time it was, and then he would go and look at the kitchen clock.

And then it was October 1987, and with it, our financial crisis. That was Black October, when there was a sudden, severe, and largely unexpected market crash that struck the global financial market system. The value of stocks and shares declined rapidly during the following five days, and selling pressure hit a peak on October 19, known as Black Monday! Unfortunately, Reggie panicked, sold out right at the bottom, and lost over 50% of his assets. Eventually, the stock market recovered, but Reggie didn't. We did not have any way of working towards recovering our money. And this is why, in hindsight, it would have been a good investment to buy that guest house. But, of course, we did not have a Crystal Ball to see the future.

Reggie went into a deep depression, but did not want to get help from anybody, least of all a therapist. He didn't want to do anything at all, not even pick up the kids. Reggie spent his days reading a couple of newspapers, or just staring at the fire in the stove. He lost his will to live. I could understand him up to a point as he was worried about our future. We still had enough money to get a business, but he did not want that. I was 34 years old, and full of enthusiasm to do some work, especially if I could do it from home.

Reggie started to complain about everything in England, especially the weather. Finally, he told me he could not stand it any longer and he wanted us all to move back to Argentina. I couldn't believe it. William was making such good progress at school and he was happy there, the teachers knew how to help him, and we also got the support we needed. I knew I was not going to be able to get a similar school in Cordoba. Roderick was also very settled at school and had a few good friends. Reggie convinced me he could get another contract to export butterflies, and we could do very well with this business, especially as the rate of exchange £/ ARG $ was well in our favour once more. I do regret not having been more assertive as this was very selfish of him!

Reggie was adamant about going back. To top up his decision, there was also the scare from the Chernobyl disaster in 1986. Finally, we put our house for sale, and started organising our things to move back to Argentina.

At the end of February 1988, we moved back. We put everything in a 40-foot container, just as we had done when we left Argentina, and off we went. We spent two days in London, and our flight was London/Caracas/ Buenos Aires/Cordoba. One day we were with the kids in a park in London, and William was jumping from a low wall. He was having a lot of fun, but in one of those jumps he hit his head against a low branch that had been pruned and was sharp. William started to bleed badly from the cut on his forehead. We took a taxi and went to the nearest hospital where they put a couple of stitches. This was done without anaesthesia, with William wrapped in a blanket so that he could not move. Poor thing, he was screaming at the top of his voice!

The flight to Caracas was good, and we booked into a hotel for two nights. As usual, the weather in Caracas was very hot and humid, too hot to go sightseeing, so we spent all day in the swimming pool. The hospital in London had given me a bandage for William's head....so I bandaged his head before getting into the pool to prevent any water getting to the stitches. It worked, but William was not very happy with it as he could not jump in and go under the water.

The flight from Caracas to Buenos Aires was uneventful, and then we arrived in Cordoba.

William loved the flight and the stay at the hotel. We had talked about moving back to Argentina, and he was looking forward to seeing Analia and Barbara, jumping into the pool, and going for walks. He didn't seem to mind the change at all, or leaving his school.

We had arranged with our friends, The Guells, that they were going to lend us their summer house in Villa Silvina until we could buy a house. I will always be grateful for this gesture, and it turned out very useful indeed!

Chapter Four

Salsipuedes

I didn't want to buy a house in Villa Silvina again, it was a bit isolated, and I had to drive everywhere. I went to see an Estate Agent in Salsipuedes and the owner told me he had his own house for sale in the village. I fell in love with the house the minute I saw it, and when I showed it to Reggie, he liked it as well. The house was very well situated, about 200 metres from the High St and the main shops. It was called "El Cortijo" as it had been built in a Spanish style. It had a veranda surrounding the house, in an L shape. It had three bedrooms upstairs, a bathroom, and an open terrace. Downstairs, there was a toilet, a biggish lounge-dining room, a good size kitchen with a big breakfast room, and a huge garage. The garage was long, with enough room for three cars. At the back of the garage, there was a separate bedroom and bathroom, the "Live-in maid's quarters". There was also a small laundry room. The house had lovely floor tiles, and old-style washbasins in the toilets.

There was a big swimming pool in the garden and a thatched BBQ area. There were two wells in the garden, one at the bottom of it that produced all the water for the swimming pool. The other well, at the top of the garden, was to provide water for the house, but we never used it as there was running water. At the bottom of the garden, there were some steps leading to a stream that ran through the town. The land was sloping. From the street, to the bottom of the garden, there was quite a drop. The back of the house was elevated, and there were steps from the veranda down. Under the garage, there was a tool room, and under the veranda, there was another biggish room. It was in this room that Reggie set up his butterfly breeding project.

All in all, it was the perfect setting.

Our house in Salsipuedes

Finally, our container arrived with all our things. The kids were happy to see their own toys and everything they had in Tavistock. William was happy to see his Fisher-Price record player. Fortunately, he had grown out of "the bit that goes inside" and, while still at the Guell's house in Villa Silvina, William had started using the video camera and was filming here and there all day long. Once we moved into our own house, William carried on doing this and also listening to music. William seemed happy with the change and he was more settled. I was really surprised how well he reacted to all the changes. As long as all the family was together William seemed to go along with the flow and was happy to move from one country to another, and from one house to a new one.

We decided to send Roderick to the local school so that he could make local friends, and this proved to be a good move. There was a kid, just up the road, that was in his class, and they walked to school together and became good friends.

The main problem was finding a suitable school for William. I knew I was not going to find a school like Gulworthy, for children with autism. A friend told me that there was a new school for children with special needs in Rio Ceballos, the town where the kids had attended nursery school. It was called America Latina, and the headteacher, Margarita, seemed to be a person with common sense, and happy to take William in. Margarita told me she had experience with autistic children, and this made me feel a bit more at ease. So, both kids started their new school year.

William was happy in his new school, and was doing many activities there including some gardening, or so I was told. That year was quite good but, towards the end, I realised that William was only listening to music and not too much more. This was quite disappointing as I had hoped his new school would help him with his development! Another blow of many, but resilient me was not going to let myself down, and I, once more, started looking for another school.

That was our first summer in our house, and we were quite busy. Reggie started breeding butterflies, I would help him as much as possible, but there was not a lot of space for both of us in the breeding room. Roderick had made a lot of friends in the neighbourhood and every day they came to the swimming pool. This was good, in a way, as William was included in the jumping and pushing games in the water. On the other hand, every day I provided all the kids with chocolate milk, biscuits, and towels. So, the following summer, I told them they were all invited to the pool but, at 5pm they all had to go back home for afternoon tea, then they could come back, with towels or otherwise dry up in the sunshine.

That summer was a good season for butterflies, and Reggie made some money and was happy.

Picnic

In March 1989, Roderick, aged 9, started at the German School (Colegio Aleman), a trilingual school in Arguello, 40 km from our house, north of the city of Cordoba. This school was in Spanish in the morning and English and German in the afternoon. It was a private school and very expensive, but an excellent one. Roderick finished high-school there in 1999.

As I was very disappointed with Escuela America Latina, I started looking for another school for William. I was told of a good private school, Instituto Alzogaray, for special needs children, not far from Roderick's school. This was run by a psychologist and had a good reputation. It was mainly a school for children with neurological and physical problems. William started going there in March when he was 10 years old. I used to drop Roderick at 8am, then William, and picked them up at 4pm. There were other kids, not far from home, going to the German School, and with their parents, we had designed a rota for taking and picking up the kids.

William was happy at his school and seemed to be improving. There was an excellent teacher there, Aurora Sanz, who used music-therapy to work with him, and had very good results. Aurora realised that William's thinking was not in the same frequency or structured in the same way as the rest of the children. Basically, William's brain was wired in a different way. Something I had been saying all along, but nobody wanted to accept it. It felt really good to have found somebody that understood William as he was, and how I felt. Aurora worked well with William, and we became good friends. Sometimes William went to Aurora's house and spent the night there. Aurora's children were a bit older than William and went along with William's way of relating to people. William really enjoyed his time at Aurora's.

Instituto Alzogaray was good for William, and he improved a lot there. It was also a boarding school, and William stayed there twice when I could not cope with him. William didn't mind and told me he had enjoyed it.

Aurora, apart from teaching at the Institute, was a Doctor in Philosophy and wrote a book with a chapter dedicated to William, and the ethics of teaching children with special needs.

Here are some of the ideas I copied from her book (with her permission), together with some of my own comments. Aurora's comments are in italics, and mine in standard text.

"When William started at the Institute, he went to a corner and just licked his knee, played with a calculator, or went to a climbing frame in the playground and shouted swear words". William is slow to accept changes, and he had the major change of moving from Tavistock to Salsipuedes, changing school from Gulworthy to America Latina, and now another school change. When William was anxious, he liked to lick his knee, or chew the top of his T-shirt. Shouting swear words was his way of attracting attention to see what happened and how everybody reacted.

When William is anxious, he plays with his tongue

Aurora was already using music-therapy with some of the other children, and little by little, through hearing the music in the classroom, William decided to go in. Aurora gave William the time he needed to start trusting her, and after a while he was happy to participate in some activities. Aurora realised that William prioritised sounds oversight, and that although he might appear to be in his own little world, he was paying attention to the sounds around him. This is something that I have mentioned before, that although William was in his own world, he was listening to what we were talking about, and if it was about him, he appeared upset.

I have already mentioned that clocks, and time, were important to William. "William wanted to know what time he was going to be picked up by his mum and asked what time it was many times during the day. He also wanted to have a fixed time for his activities. He would ask how long he would have to be working on any particular task. He would not accept an answer such as: for a while, during the morning, for a short time, for some time, or until I told you to stop. All these were ambiguous replies, and he wanted to know exactly how long: 5 minutes, an hour, etc."

William has always been like that, no grey areas, things are black or white, nothing in the middle. It calms him down to know how long something will take to resolve. This is very important to understand as it has a calming effect to address "black and white" activities, answers, and items.

For some time, starting in Tavistock, William had been able to do calculations in his head, even complicated ones, mainly related to time. Unfortunately, he was never been able to apply it to real life. Even if he knows the answer, if one wrote a math calculation on paper, he would either give the wrong answer or just won't bother to do it. But if it was related to time, days, months, years, he could instantly do the calculation in his head and in seconds tell you the answer.

It was at this time that we realised that he could tell us the day of the week of any given date. And it started with birthdays, and friends would ask him on what day of the week they were born, and he would tell them the right answer. We started checking with days in the past, and in the future, and William would always give the right answer. This was before the internet, but we had The World Almanac and Book of Facts, and we could check the dates and days there. We have never been able to understand this Savant ability, and how he copes with leap years. I guess it all has to do with patterns.

Aurora was able to work with him doing some sums, and other calculations. William learnt how to read and write in Spanish. The main achievement was to be able to sit down to do an activity, for the established time, and finish it.

William started to find a pattern of routines and activities. He made progress integrating with the staff and the other pupils. He wanted to know why some of the pupils could not talk, see or walk. But he also wanted to know when they would be able to walk, see or talk. He was almost fascinated by the problems other children had, and wanted to know when they would be cured.

Aurora realised that William's relationship with the outer world was a sum of parts, times, fixed structures, patterns. Knowing the time an activity or a task will take to get completed, reassured him that he would be able to go back to his own world, even if it was for a short time. Panic set in when he didn't know when he could be in his own place and inner world again. This is still the same. He would choose to come out of his world if he thought he was going to enjoy it, knowing he could stop it at any time. His logic suggested that coming out of his world was highly risky, and he needed to be sure he could return to his own world. It is very important to respect his times, when he wants to retreat to his inner self, not to push him too hard to come out, but let him choose when to do it. It is all right to encourage him to come out, but also to let him know you are there for him when he chooses to do it.

For many years, William spoke in the third person. His identity was not established. He would say: William doesn't want to take a bath, referring to himself. Aurora helped him to establish his identity up to a point, or as much as he let her do it. Although now, in 2020, he speaks in the first person when he refers to himself, he still finds it difficult to tell stories that happened to him, or that he would like to have happened to him, with his name as the main character. For example, he will tell a story, but instead of William being the main character, it is Oliver Twist, or some other child that went to school with him. He also replaces himself with the dog. This dog hasn't got a name, it is just the dog.

"Once William learnt to read and write in Spanish, he made up a game where he would replace a word, in a sentence, for another word that would not make any sense, and wanting to know the meaning of the sentence with this new word. He would also replace a letter in a word, wanting to know the meaning of the word he had made up.

"At the end of the school year, William's father came to pick him up, and wanted to see what William had been doing during that year. I showed him the notebooks with William's Maths, and also what William had been writing. I told Reggie that William had learnt to read and write in Spanish, and that through music I had been helping him to come out of his inner world and learnt to accept tasks that could be enjoyable to him. Unfortunately, Reggie could not accept that William was different, and he was very disappointed with our work with William. Reggie had expected that William could start learning some trade, or something that he would be able to apply to a job in the future."

Roderick, in the meantime, settled well in Colegio Aleman, and made many friends. He has always been a very bright, clever boy, and he took full advantage of his education in this school.

Reggie had made friends with a German guy in Salsipuedes, Stefan Wolpe, a very nice person, quite a bit older than Reggie. They used to get together once or twice a week to play chess.

We made friends with a couple who owned a very old property in Salsipuedes. His land had been in his family since the 1600s, and he belonged to one of the traditional families in Cordoba, the equivalent to the aristocracy! Jorge Maldonado was a well-established solicitor and a very nice person. Jorge used to come and visit us whenever he was in Salsipuedes. Reggie and Jorge had some interesting talks about politics, history, etc. Reggie's Spanish was quite good in a one-to-one conversation, but he had difficulty in a group as it is normal in Argentina to talk all at the same time, interrupt, or talk across somebody else.

We were close with my uncle and aunt, Edwin and Betty, who lived in Unquillo. We used to invite them over for dinner or get together at their house. They spoke perfect English, and both Reggie and I enjoyed their company. I tried to socialise as much as possible with people Reggie felt comfortable with, and we did this as a couple. I also met with my friends and cousins as much as possible. Reggie was quite happy when my whole extended family came for a BBQ or gathering, but soon after lunch, he would go inside to be on his own. If the older generation was there, and by this, I mean uncles or aunts of similar age group to Reggie, then he would sit with them at the table and he was all right. This marked, even more, our differences in age and interests. But he didn't mind if people came, he would join in for a while and then got bored as he could not follow the conversations. It was a pity as Reggie had been very sociable in Scotland.

The house was lovely but very cold in winter. The garage was like a freezer and we put our coats on when we went there. The piano, Reggie's roll-top desk, and our bookshelves were there. A joiner made us some very long shelves, and we put all our books there, plus a collection of National Geographic magazines that Reggie had been accumulating for years, and still had the subscription while we lived in Salsipuedes.

There was a fireplace in the lounge which was kept on all day long when it was cold. There was also a fireplace at the end of the corridor upstairs, next to the bathroom. This fireplace was useless. The firewood had to be carried upstairs, and the draft was so powerful that it consumed the firewood quickly but did not make the place any warmer.

There was a small heater in the corridor, under the stained-glass window. This also proved quite useless as the heat would go out of the window. All in all, it was very cold upstairs, but the winters don't last very long in Cordoba, and we just wrapped up to go to bed, had warm quilts and blankets.

That winter, 1989, was not very good. Reggie was quite low; he would not accept William's autism. He kept saying we should have been stricter with him, and he did not cope well when William had a meltdown. Unless he was playing chess with Stefan, Reggie spent his winter days reading the newspaper and complaining about all the things that were wrong with Argentina. This was putting a lot of stress on our marriage. It is not easy, for a couple, to cope with an autistic son, it either pulls you closer, or breaks you apart. Unless you both pull in the same direction, a problem like autism could easily break your marriage. Our problems started in Tavistock, after the stock market crash. But in Salsipuedes our marriage deteriorated further.

When the autumn came, I suggested to Reggie that it would be a good idea to buy a computer and do a bit of research on how other people were dealing with their butterfly breeding, and it would also be good to research about autism.

We bought a computer and got connected to the internet. This was new technology and very exciting. This was a great improvement for all of us, even William learnt how to use it. William loved to use the typewriter and spent hours typing calendars. He also used the computer to make calendars.

The summer arrived (1990), and Reggie started breeding butterflies again. Unfortunately, it did not go very well. Reggie was not careful with hygiene, there were too many larvae in a confined space, and they were getting infections. The larvae were not protected against parasites, and the pupae sent to London hatched, but instead of butterflies, they got parasites. Reggie was very stubborn and would not accept his errors. He worked hard that summer but did not make any money. And this story repeated itself during the following summers. I contacted, on their website, The International Butterfly Breeders Association, and kept telling Reggie about the methods they were using to protect the larvae, and how important hygiene was. Reggie kept telling me he had been breeding butterflies all his life and there was nothing new to learn. And all summers, from then on, were the same...a lot of work for Reggie but with very poor results, and practically no income. This was no good for Reggie's morale. If Reggie was low it affected the whole family.

William kept telling me some stories that happened to him, with their corresponding dates, and I will transcribe them here as he has told them to me.

There was a small supermarket in Rio Ceballos called Atea. It belonged to a man called Tito Atea, and it had an excellent delicatessen department. The butcher had first-class meat. William loved to go to this supermarket. One day we were there early, just before they opened. When Tito Atea went in, the first thing he did was to disconnect the alarm. He didn't notice, neither did I, that William was behind him. Cheeky boy, he had memorised the code, and later on, he went and connected it while customers were in, and the alarm went off!

William tells the story that on the 8th of April 1989, while I was buying some meat, and the butcher was weighing it on the scales. William was touching the scales and the butcher was getting upset. I smacked his hand, and when we were in the car, he hit me in the face. I hit him back and we both started to cry. I vaguely remember this.

On the 29th of April, the same year, same place, Supermercado Atea, he lost his watch. We looked around but we could not find it. William was crying, and he said I told him not to worry because we could go and buy another one....and so we did. He had the bad habit of carrying his watch in his hand instead of around his wrist.

The school year started in March with both kids at their own schools. William appeared to be happy at Instituto Alzogaray.

Continuing with some of Aurora's views on William. She said that it was as if William "was "filming" life, from the outside like a camera, a viewfinder and microphone that recorded parts, moments, places, selected parts of the reality, a sequence of images, and feelings, but that didn't have the same speed to cause him vertigo...as he himself had selected them....a spectator separated from the reality of the world.

Traditional education follows a logic of IQ tests, achieving values and structures, categories, and patterns designed for "normal" standards, in a pre-established order. William had a different rhythm and working with him was a challenge to go at his own pace. Objects, people, and activities, don't have a place in his world, they affect his world. The world, as we know it, with a common structure that defines objects and actions with an established idea, is not attractive to William, or something he should pay attention to, or get involved in.

The world was there, and William was here, and he could not integrate both. Being in the world, participating with others, was frightening for William. William couldn't cope with certain things like a power cut, that happened quite often, or losing something. He would go into a tantrum like a two-year-old child. This put a lot of pressure on the whole family as it was very distressing".

Roderick had friends over at weekends, or he would go to his friends in Cordoba. Every Sunday my parents came to visit us and although it was lovely to see them, they were not making too much progress with William. This was very sad for my parents and for myself. It was very hard for them, and they meant well, but they didn't understand they had to relate to William in his terms, they wanted William to come out of his shell and "become normal".

Quite frequently, on a Saturday, I used to take William across the hills to a hamlet called Los Cocos, near La Cumbre, an old British settlement. The road to Los Cocos was a very windy dirt road with magnificent views. We both liked the drive to Los Cocos. The purpose of these trips was to go to the chairlift. William would go up and down about 5 or 6 times, and he got some thrill from being elevated to the top and down. I just sat at the bottom and watched him going up and down.

Whenever we were in the car, William wanted the radio on to listen to music. He wanted to know if the other cars had radios as well. This became an obsession, and for a long time, while in the car, as other cars went past, he would ask me if they had a radio. If I was concentrating on the traffic, and didn't answer immediately, he would grab my chin and make me look at the car in question. William always sat in the back seat and he would grab me from behind, which was extremely dangerous.

In 1990, when William was 11, he had hepatitis A and had to rest for 20 days. He tells the story that we went to the hospital to have a blood test, and then we went to Buenos Aires to have another blood test. He told me we took the coach to Buenos Aires, went walking to the hotel, and stayed there for three nights. He went up and down the stairs many times and he was happy. I don't remember this at all, but it must be true if he remembers it. What sounds odd to me is that if he had hepatitis and had to rest, I wouldn't have let him go up and down the stairs. And why have a blood test in Buenos Aires. But William's memory is not to be doubted!

If not at school, William spent most of his time listening to music, filming with the video camera, or looking at books. He had his own books he liked to read, mostly children's stories, or reference books. He had a collection of books called The Earth, The Rain, The Fire, The Weather, The Water, The Solar System, and The Seasons. He also liked to look at the many Atlases of the world, at books of British villages, and also at dictionaries. Reggie had several dictionaries of different languages, German, Italian, Portuguese, etc., and William loved to look up words in different languages. He learnt many words in other languages, and he had fun doing this.

William was very careful with the cassettes, and long-playing records, and he always put them back in the correct box or cover. I had lots of ornaments, but William never touched them, and he never broke anything.

William has always had a different sensitivity to sensations of cold, heat, pain, and sounds, as normally experienced. It could be very cold, and he would be in a T-shirt, or very hot and be wearing a sweatshirt. He might have been in pain, but he didn't complain. This behaviour has remained the same since he was a child.

William, who was 11 years old, was eating well and accepted most foods. He had some fixations with some foods but, mostly, he ate what he was given. I had noticed that some food preferences had to do with texture or colour. He loved salads, mostly lettuce and tomatoes, always with a lot of salt, vinegar, and oil. Pasta has always been one of his favourites...the same consistency regardless of the variety. Food with pastry. Strawberries: red, as tomatoes. Bananas, because of the creamy brown similarity to pasta. Given the choice, he would eat these foods every day. This again has remained constant during his lifetime.

Another constant aspect in his life has been his reaction to anything new, especially clothes or shoes. If we bought him any new item of clothing, it had to be in his wardrobe for a couple of weeks before he would consider wearing it. Again, since childhood he would not wear it straight away.

William kept shouting when he had his haircut. Fortunately, Vilma, my longlife friend who was a hairdresser, always cut his hair and we just laughed afterwards, as he reacted as if he had been tortured. I feel very grateful to Vilma as she cut William's hair for many years. Eventually, he started to accept his haircut trips to Vilma's house as normality. Vilma has always been a good friend to me since we were teenagers, and we met up regularly. William started to relate well to Vilma as she shared his sense of humour and his games. Vilma has also been a moral support to me, and a good listener to my problems.

That summer my parents, my sister and her family, had planned to go camping to a camping site in Los Reartes, not far from Villa General Belgrano, the place where William had become toilet trained. They had been there before, and to me it sounded like a good place to go. Reggie didn't like camping, so I went with both kids. Roderick shared a small tent with his cousin Martin, one of my sister's sons. The camping site was by a big river, with deep pools to swim in. William loved to be in the enclosed space of the tent (which he shared with me), and he loved the river. There were some big rocks in the river and all the kids would jump in from there. My sister's kids, three sons and a daughter, related well to William, on William's own terms. We all had our meals together and played cards after dinner. William was quite happy to go back to the tent after dinner, and either he slept early, or was quite content in the dark confined space of the tent.

William was not embarrassed to come out of the tent naked. In fact, he has never seen any reason why he could not be naked in front of other people. It took me many years to teach him this was not always appropriate. Even now, in 2020, he might come out of his room in his underpants and answer the front door if the postman rings the bell.

There were separate showers for ladies and gents. When I was in the shower, and William wanted to talk to me, he would just walk in and start opening all the shower curtains until he found me. To begin with, the other ladies were a bit shocked, but they soon accepted that it was just William who would look at them but not see their nakedness. For William, a piece of furniture or these ladies was the same. I must say that William is completely asexual, and he is not interested in seeing anybody naked.

Our campsite was small, and family orientated. Everybody was friendly and very understanding. We went for long walks, and sometimes we went shopping or for a meal to Villa General Belgrano. As afternoons are very hot in the Province of Cordoba, we used to have a siesta after lunch. William was happy to stay confined in the tent. One day there was a very bad storm with a lot of rain, the river was swollen into a torrent. The following day we could not go to the river as it was dangerous, but William could not understand this and had a terrible tantrum that lasted all day long. There was no way of calming him down. It was not pleasant for anybody in our group, or the people in the nearby tents. Fortunately, the following day the river had returned to normal and William was happy.

His cousins had endless fun asking William different dates and getting the right day of the week. They also had fun asking William if such a person was a man or a woman, William never got it right, he could not tell the difference. On many occasions, we tried to teach him the difference, pointing out the hair length, the way of dressing, but it was not easy as there were so many similarities, and he couldn't relate to breasts or body shapes. If we talked about somebody and referred to that person as a lady, or as a man, he would only know by repetition, but not because he could tell the difference. This was a great source of enjoyment for the kids, and William didn't mind going along with this.

So, all in all, William enjoyed his two weeks camping.

There was a Lido in Salsipuedes, and William started going there to swim. He loved to be with the other kids on the diving board, and the kids would push him into the water. Most summers he went there twice a week. One day, while he was swimming, he saw that a little girl was in distress at the bottom of the pool. William pulled her out and saved her from drowning.

121

The parents were very grateful, and the girl sent him a letter to thank him.

The letter says thanks for helping me when I needed it. my family and I are very grateful. god bless you and help you in your life. thanks.

March 1991 was the start of a new big problem. The kids started their school year at the beginning of March, and they were both happy to start their daily routine. William was still working with Aurora, and some other teachers.

The economy in Argentina has always been a roller coaster, with good years and then crashing. At that time, the inflation was very high, and the economy was in a complete mess. The economy has always been linked to the dollar, and the higher the inflation the value of the dollar went higher as well. For us it had always worked in our favour as we had hard currency. To counteract the inflation, the government decided to implement what they called Plan de Convertibilidad, where the Argentine Peso and the dollar had the same value: 1ARP$ = 1U$S. This was a terrible situation for us as our income went down and, in reality, we could only afford our food but nothing else. We started to live on capital and Reggie started selling stocks and shares. It was a very worrying situation. I got a job in Academia

Arguello, a bilingual school in Arguello, not far from the kids' school. I worked there in the afternoon. In the morning the students had their subjects in Spanish, and English in the afternoons. The salary was not great, but it helped.

Since we moved in, in 1988, I had a maid that came every day to help me with the housework. Liliana used to previously come to Villa Silvina when we lived there. She knew the kids very well and was patient and affectionate with William. We had to cut down on her days and she only came once a week. The house was big, and in the autumn, the veranda gathered a lot of autumn leaves that had to be swept every day. It was a lot of work on top of my everyday job.

This situation just drove Reggie into a deeper depression, and he started to drink a lot of whisky. He didn't get drunk, but it got him into a bad mood and became very heavy in his arguments. It was hard to get home and find him in such a cantankerous mood, his dirty porridge pot and bowl still in the sink, the housework to do, dinner to cook, William's problems to cope with, and having to listen to a list of complaints about Argentina (mostly true) that became a daily repetition. Don't get me wrong, it takes two to tango, and I accept my part of the responsibility. Reggie was a good person, and he had been a lot of fun, but circumstances changed him completely. I think the main problem in our marriage was the big difference in age, 23 years is a bit much. My parents had warned me about this, but I didn't pay any attention. I was in love, and we had spoken about this with Reggie, and decided that even if we were happy for ten years it was worth it. The problem was that after ten years, he would not accept that unless he made an effort to keep busy and young in mind and spirit, the difference in age was going to be more noticeable as time went on.

We could have changed Roderick's education to a local school, and saved the fees of the Colegio Aleman, but we considered that Roderick deserved the best education we could provide. It was not easy for Roderick to cope with William's problems, and with parents who did not get on well. It would have been very unfair to him to change his school. Roderick had a very nice group of school friends, which was good for him, and I guess gave him the moral support he needed to cope with the problems he had to face at home.

I begged Reggie to consider coming back to the UK, but he would not have it. Reggie said he would not be able to cope with the weather, and that he would not be happy at all in the UK. Reggie had become very selfish and only thought about himself. I knew that Roderick would be able to cope with life anywhere in the world, and he would be able to get a great education in England, and a better future. For William life in England would be much better, and I would be able to get the support I needed. Reggie agreed to put the house for sale, knowing that the Real Estate business was dead at that time.

And so, life continued with its ups and downs, and Reggie and I grew further apart. I was out working all day, had a lot to do when I went back home, and on Sundays my parents came for a visit….and so life went on.

From a young age, if anybody kissed William or touched him, he would immediately touch the spot. It was like he was cleaning the spot where he had been kissed, or touched, or putting his own "touch" to that spot. It was like making sure there was nothing remaining of that person on his body or himself, and by touching it himself he was a

125

whole person again. We started calling this action "tocadura", meaning his own touch. This has remained with him through the years and he still does it. As part of the same "syndrome", when he gets his food served at home, or at a restaurant, he touches it all around with his fork. If he gets a sandwich, biscuit, or any other finger food, he first touches it all around, like marking his territory! He does the same with his glass or mug, he will add his mark to it. William doesn't like to be touched, hugged or kissed. Even when he was a baby, he didn't get comfort from a cuddle, or felt soothed from being held tight. Looking back, I think William used to cry a lot when he was a baby, because being comforted by cuddling distressed him, but he couldn't tell me. The more I held him tight, rocked him, and tried to calm him down in my arms, the more he cried. When he started walking and could escape from my arms, he was happier. He chose when to be closer, like sitting on my lap to play "galloping on a horse", or rough and tumble games.

Another of William's stories, and I quote, is that on the 28th of July 1991, he was in the bedroom and Roderick wanted to get something and put the light on, William got up and switched it off, so Roderick opened the shutter and William started to shout and cry. Apparently, according to his story, I told him to come with me and I was going to lock him up in the bathroom, but he then stopped crying and accepted having the shutter opened.

Another story is that on the 28th of September 1991, Reggie was reading a book, William came and grabbed it from his hands and Reggie got annoyed and smacked his hand, and William started crying.

All his stories have some drama in them and amuse him no end.

Sometime that year, I started giving William more independence. I thought it would be good to concentrate on the activities he could do, and he felt confident, rather than feeling scared than something bad was going to happen to him. Salsipuedes was, back then, a small village and everybody knew us, and William. William started walking by himself to two different bakers. The owners of these two shops were very good with William, and he liked going there. He always got a bun, or a biscuit, and this encouraged him to go back. He talked to the owners who were very patient with him. As everybody knew William, I felt he was safe, and they would tell me if William was in any danger.

At the bottom of our garden: steps down to the river

When spring came and the weather was warmer, William would go down the steps to the river to walk along the bank for a short while. A short distance from our bottom gate, there was a "balneario", a man-made swimming pool in the river, with a sluice that was open in the winter, or to clean the pool, and closed in the summer to let the pool fill up. One spring the sluice was half-open, and there was a lot of water in the river as it had been raining a lot. William was a good swimmer and he asked to go to the river to swim. Roderick went with him. There was a parking attendant to look after the pool. William, always looking for something contradictory to try, started to swim from the pool down the river, going under the sluice. The park attendant told him off a few times as he was afraid William could get stuck under the sluice and drown. But, as usual, once William had made up his mind, the more one told him not to do something, the more he wanted to do it. And if he was told that something was dangerous, this was a great encouragement for him to try it harder to see the outcome. Eventually, the park attendant gave up and just watched him. Roderick was there and he would have acted fast if William had been in danger. He is like a cat; he has nine lives. William has been, and always is, in dangerous situations that he chooses to be in, and always comes out smelling of roses.

William continued having tantrums, meltdowns, shouting, and being very anxious every time he lost something, or the electricity was off. On top of his normal frustrations, he was growing up and had to cope with his teenage hormones.

Another of his favourite stories, and I quote, is that on the 21st of March 1992 he was shouting and having a meltdown as the electricity had gone off. There had been a bad storm on the night of the 20th, and several trees had been blown down and some cables got cut. His meltdown was so bad that I took him to Instituto Alzogaray and he spent the night there. I was glad to have the possibility of taking William to the Instituto as it gave me some kind of respite and it was well appreciated.

He also loves the story, and he talks about it quite frequently, when one evening Reggie had gone to the shops, and when he was walking back home a dog bit him on his leg. When he arrived home, he sat on the edge of the bath and washed his leg under the tap. I called the paramedics, they disinfected the wound, and gave him anti-rabies treatment. (Again, a story with a drama). William observed the whole procedure and was very interested in the injections.

William loved the weather in Cordoba. Winters are dry, with very cold mornings and nights, but it could be 20C or more in the afternoon. Summers are very hot, with days getting hotter and hotter until there is a big thunderstorm, torrential rain, and then the sun comes out again. William liked the storms, watching the lightning, listening to the

130

thunder, but he didn't like the consequences which often ended in a power cut. These power cuts could last between a couple of hours to 24 hours. As soon as the power was off, he wanted me to phone the Electricity Company (EPEC) to ask them when they were going to restore the power. It was useless phoning them as they had a big rural area to cover, and they were doing the best to get the electricity back. I just made out that I was phoning them, and always told William that they were going to take 24 hours. Remember that William has never accepted an ambiguous answer. He wanted to know how many hours, and so I told him longer than expected, and if it was connected earlier that was a bonus. But then, as he became older and had more independence to go around Salsipuedes, he wanted to go and look for the EPEC lorry to ask the men himself. Sometimes he succeeded in finding them, and the men soon learnt to tell him a longer period than expected.

Reggie bought the newspaper every day, and William asked me to cut out the weather forecast, and he stuck it in his current notebook. He was always writing in a copybook, and had started to follow the weather forecast every day. The problem was that he thought that the newspaper was

131

actually IN CHARGE of the weather. If the weather forecast said that it was going to be cloudy, William wanted me to phone the newspaper and tell them to change it to be sunny. It took him many years to learn that the newspapers had nothing to do with the weather and they were only reporting on it.

This is another of his stories related to the weather. (And I quote) It was cloudy on the night of 21st of July 1993, and William could not see Jupiter and he had an awful meltdown, crying and shouting because he wanted to see it. It was cloudy for another two nights, and the same happened every night. On the fourth day, according to William, we were both in the garden, and I was watering. William started to go on and on about Jupiter, and I hit him with the garden hose on his legs and he stopped shouting. But on the 7th of August it was cloudy again and that night William could not see Jupiter and another meltdown took place. William likes to tell this story even now, in 2020, and apparently, when I went to pick him up the following day, from Instituto Alzogaray, I told Juan Manuel, the manager, that William had been naughty.

In Argentina, everybody has an ID card that is issued at birth and needs to be renewed at fourteen and at 18 years old. William became fourteen on Feb 11th, 1993. As usual, in Argentina, this involved a lot of paperwork, signatures, official stamping, etc. Even more so as William was British, with Argentinian citizenship. We had to make an appointment for signing all the paperwork, and two weeks later to collect it. William had to sign in thirteen different places, which he dutifully did in 12 places, but for his 13th signature, he signed Edith Piaf, his favourite singer at the time. He laughed loudly as this seemed very funny to him. You don't mess about with government officials but, fortunately, and by coincidence, we had met the agent once at a friend's party. He agreed to apply Tippex to Edith Piaf, and William signed again William Elliott. He laughed all the way home at his "joke". We then had an appointment, two weeks later, to pick up his new ID card. This required another signature, by William, in the booklet itself. The ID, at that time, was a booklet like a small passport. The waiting room was very crowded, and we sat down to wait for our number to be called. I was afraid that William would sign Edith Piaf again. While we were waiting, I said to William,

133

"If you sign Edith Piaf instead of William Elliott, I'll kill you." People with autism take everything in a literal way, unless they have learnt that what you are saying is not to be taken at face value. So, right in the middle of the crowded room, William started to shout, "Please don't kill me, nooo, don't kill me!" I was laughing and had to explain to him that it was a way of saying I would be very upset! We got his ID card and he signed the correct name. And he learnt that if I said I was going to kill him, it meant I would be upset. This is another story for his collection.

We used to go horse-riding, with Nestor and family, to an Estancia (big farm/ranch) some 2km off from the main dual carriageway to Cordoba. We got to know the owners quite well and visited each other from time to time. Somehow, William enjoyed going to this Estancia called Santo Domingo. The Estancia had a big, natural pond into which the Salsipuedes river drained. William worked out that if he went walking along the river, from our house, he could reach the pond. Going along with giving him more independence and letting him do whatever he felt really confident in doing, one day he set out on his trip. We had agreed that he would go there and come back as soon as he reached the pond. We also agreed that he would walk only along the river and would not get into the "monte" (bush). I was quite anxious as there were many poisonous snakes in that area. William took an hour to reach the boundary of the Estancia, but he didn't cross the fence as he could hear dogs barking. The pond was not far from the fence, but he was quite happy to see it from behind the fence. The return trip took him two hours. This became a regular activity, which he enjoyed tremendously, and, fortunately, without any apparent hazards.

Knowing about the hazards of living in a rural area, I've always kept an EpiPen (a Decadron injection) in case of snake bite while waiting for paramedics to arrive and inject antivenom.

One morning, William went out on his walking trip to Santo Domingo, and we checked our watches. Knowing he would take exactly two hours and not a minute more, or less, I carried on with whatever I was doing. Two hours went past, another ten minutes, and I started to get anxious. After 20 minutes I asked Roderick to accompany me to look for William. I put the EpiPen, bandages, alcohol, and water in my backpack, and we set off. After a ten-minute walk, we saw William coming towards us, safe and happy. When we asked him why he had taken so long and what he had been doing, in his own wording he said: I was just hanging around. I was annoyed, and amused at the same time, and mostly happy that he had not been bitten by a snake, a dog, or had an encounter with a puma.

In the spring, my sister and family came for a weekend. William asked permission to go down to the river for a short walk. We fixed the time to 15 minutes and off he went. After ten minutes he came up the steps shouting and crying. He had seen a swarm of bees on the trunk of a tree and he got a long stick and hit the bees to see what would happen. The angry bees attacked him, and he was stung all over his body. Just as well my brother in law, Carlos, who is a doctor, was there and reacted quickly. William's eyes and hands were very swollen, and his throat was closing. Carlos injected him with an EpiPen and started an anti-allergic treatment every 4 hours. William recovered after 4 days.

Another story William likes to tell is, and I quote, that on the 24th of May 1994, William and Reggie had gone to the Shopping Centre. I was recovering from a keyhole gallbladder surgery, and they had gone to do some shopping to give me some peace. William doesn't like it when he finds a locked door that says, "Only for staff", or similar, or when there is an obstacle that doesn't let him go through. If it is not allowed William will want to do it. Apparently, there had been a minor fire on the top floor of the Shopping Centre, and there was a barrier at the bottom of the stairs preventing the public from having access to the top floor. This was like a magnet to William, and up he went. He didn't reach the top floor because two guards grabbed his arms and took him downstairs to where Reggie was waiting. They came home soon after that and William was very upset as he wanted to go to the top floor to see the damage caused by the fire. That evening he was very distressed, and he broke one of the stained-glass windows upstairs. The following day Reggie took him to Instituto Alzogaray and William stayed there that night.

Every summer we went camping to the same camping site in Los Reartes, and with the same crowd. By then, all the other families, regular campers, knew William quite well. William, now aged 14, asked me if he could go along the river to another pool. I was not all that happy about this as he would be on his own, but I agreed to it and we fixed a time for coming back. So, most days he would go along on his own and he knew he had to be back at 1pm for lunch, and in the evening, he would leave at 4pm and be back at 6pm. One evening he was delayed, and, after an hour, everybody wanted to help to look for him and we formed several search parties. One of those search parties found William coming through the woods and not along the river as he was supposed to do. He decided to walk through the woods but got lost and that's why he was delayed.

Before going into the river, William would take his shoes off, leave them on a rock and off he went to his favourite spot. One evening he came back but he could not find his shoes. He started shouting and getting more and more anxious as time went by. Finally, somebody found his shoes outside our tent. He had gone barefoot to the river and forgotten about it!

As time went by, William's meltdowns were more frequent, and it was very difficult to cope with them. It was as if he needed more stimulation, as if he was very frustrated.

I have always talked a lot to William and have tried to make him understand how the world functions, how people think and react, what is accepted and what is not appropriate. I know his brain is wired in a different way, and it is hard for him to grasp how other people think and react. By repetition, even if he does not completely understand it, he eventually accepts things and events. William is very repetitive in his language, he needs to ask something over and over, and come around to the same point through different approaches, and will keep doing this until he gets the right reply to his question. As he takes things literally, what he has learnt about one social event, is not necessarily applied or transferred to a similar one. And a clear example is an episode in a bus when he wanted a seat (mentioned later in this book).

I'm going to mention here what Dr Joseph Ledoux, a well-known American neurologist said about emotions, and I have changed it to make it into my own comment.

"In the presence of an event that the individual considers hurtful, unbearable, or overwhelming, the amygdala reacts, sending a message of crisis to the whole brain. Rational behaviour is not possible any longer, and emotions take over in an uncontrollable way. "It may explain why so much of emotional life is hard to understand with the rational mind."

When one is so overwhelmed by an event that one cannot stand it any longer, one reacts by shouting, crying, going mute, breaking something, running away, etc....in other words, by emotions. Apparently, in a person with autism, the limbic system, and the amygdala, in the brain, receive signals that make the person get into an emotional crisis before they have time to regulate those emotions.

William has always had a structured way of thinking. He put thoughts and knowledge into "boxes", or folders, within his brain. He sees patterns and details before he sees the whole picture.

I will add here something that explains really well how autistic people think:

- Autistic people think from the bottom up: this means they see the details first, while "normal people" see the concept first and details later. Example: we see a house, autistic people will see windows, doors, roof, garden, etc. We see a car, an autistic person will see tyres, lights, bonnet, bumper, etc.

- Autistic people take things literally: If we say "pull up your socks" we know what it means, but to an autistic person it means literally to pull their socks up.

It is very hard for an autistic person to see things from our perspective. They think that if they find something interesting, everybody will find it interesting as well. Because of this, interactions can seem off-putting or irritating. They might even say something hurtful, but it is not intentionally. This also makes them vulnerable to being taken advantage off, as they are socially naïve.

I think this is a brilliant way of explaining how autistic people think and behave!

◇◇◇

A friend told me about a home for youngsters with special needs called Granja Pia in a small town to the south of the city of Cordoba, two-hour drive from our house. We went to see it and it seemed like a nice place for William. They were all boys, teenagers and young men. They had farm animals and a vegetable garden. The boys worked on the farm, the food that was cooking in the kitchen smelled great, and the owners seemed like nice people. We could get help from the government to pay the fees, and they would arrange for this benefit to be paid directly to them. And so we agreed that William would start there in June. We took William there and he agreed to stay with no fuss. William was 15 years old. I think William is quite happy anywhere where he could have his music and find peace in his own world. Olga and Alberto, the owners, asked us to leave him for two weeks, with no contact, to let him settle in. This was hard for me, but it had to be done. After two weeks, on the Friday, after I finished my school day at Academia Arguello, I drove down to pick him up.

To start with I drove him there and picked him up. Then I decided to teach him how to travel by bus. The main problem was that he had to take a bus from Salsipuedes to the bus terminal in Cordoba and then take another bus to San Agustin bus terminal, get off and walk to Granja Pia, a short walk from the bus stop. The first time I went with him, and then I let him go on his own. I must say that William can orientate himself really well, and once he has been to a place he doesn't forget how to get there. Once he learns how to do something, he will carry on doing it in the same way. I got him a bus pass, and he was travelling to and from without any problems. I've always tried to encourage William to do as much as he could, and if he felt confident, he could do it, not matter how scared I feel, I let him do it. I feel this is good for his self-esteem.

From time to time they used to have parties where the families of the boys were invited. Most times I went on my own, and sometimes with Reggie. Sometimes, apart from the staff, the boys, and family members, there were people from the community of San Agustin. There would be a whole calf roasting on the BBQ, and plenty of food for everybody to enjoy.

William started saying that he wanted somebody to build a runway so he could go to Granja Pia every day and come back home by plane. He kept going on and on with this story. As he loves flying, I thought it was just a wish, and a product of his imagination. William doesn't accept no for an answer without a proper explanation. I tried to explain that it was not possible to build a runway in San Agustin and another one in Salsipuedes. Finally, as I did many times, I made up an acceptable story that kept him happy. I invented a character, Mr Rodriguez, who was going to get all the materials needed to build the runway. So, Mr Rodriguez travelled to Buenos Aires to buy "the bricks", but as he crossed the main road he was run over by a car and died. William has always accepted drastic results and it seems to put a final closure to any of the issues. And then I could not get anybody to build it. William insisted that maybe a policeman could build it, but I convinced him that policemen went chasing thieves and they did not know how to build runways. But most weekends, when William came home, he would mention the runway.

Alberto, Olga, and the staff, were planning a horse-riding trip to the town of Jesus Maria, in the north of Cordoba, to take part in a big yearly festival called "Doma y Folklore". During this festival, the "gauchos" show their horsemanship, there are groups or artists singing folk music, horses being tamed, and similar country activities. This was going to be a major adventure and challenge. The trip was going to last three days, and accommodation had to be found for the kids, staff, and horses. Food had to be considered as well. I really took my hat off to them as everything was planned to perfection. The boys had become used to the horses and had learnt to ride. The horses were very tame, and they would all go together. William came back home on the 20th of December and we thought he had to go back just after New Year on January 2nd. And this is another story that William loves retelling over and over again. Just after Christmas Alberto phoned me to let me know that I had to take William back to Granja Pia on Dec 26th, and not on the 2nd of January, as they had to practice with the horses. The festival started on January 10th, and they had to leave on the 7th. William was extremely upset at having to change the day of his return, and it was quite a struggle to take him back. Apparently, this story amuses him a lot nowadays!

Anyway, the trip was a success, and they went round and round the arena with the public clapping. William went riding part of the way, and in a cart the rest of the time. He has never felt very confident on a horse by himself. This was a great achievement not only for the boys but for the staff who organised everything. William enjoyed it all and often talks about this trip. I believe that it was a very positive event for William. Talking to the other parents, at the time of the trip, we all felt happy for the whole group, but also a bit scared as it was a somehow risky operation. The whole group was riding along a major provincial route that carried a lot of traffic. But, fortunately, the horses were very good and were used to traffic.

On the left: William on horseback

As William was used to taking the bus back and forth, to and from San Agustin, with a change in Cordoba, when he asked me if he could go to the bus terminal in Cordoba to have a coke and come back, I thought it was a good idea and would give him something to do. We agreed that he would get there, sit down to have a glass of coke, and take the bus back. I gave him the exact amount of money for the coke, some coins wrapped in masking tape. It was very successful, and he did it many times without any problems. One day he was delayed, but not for long. When he arrived, he told me he had gone to the usual restaurant, sat down and ordered his coke, plus six "empanadas" (similar to Cornish pasties). He had money only for a glass of coke. So, the waiter came with the ticket, and William told him he only had money to pay for the coke. The waiter called one of the security guards, and bless his soul, he took pity on William and paid for his empanadas. This is also a story that William finds very amusing. Obviously, I talked to him and he understood he could not do that, and that it was not appropriate, and it was the same as being a thief. (He understood it in this way...he knew about thieves and was fascinated about thieves and policemen chasing them.)

He kept going to Cordoba bus terminal for a glass of coke but always behaved properly.

William also liked to take the bus from Salsipuedes to Jesus Maria. The bus route ended there at the bus terminal. The bus driver got off, had a cup of coffee and a ten-minute rest, and drove the bus back all the way to Cordoba, stopping in the many small towns along the route, one of them Salsipuedes. The round trip took three hours. I went with William to the bus terminal, paid for his return trip, and asked the driver to keep an eye on William and make sure he was on the bus back. He did this many times that summer and in the following summers.

One day, I had a call from a shop in Ascochinga, a small town halfway between Jesus Maria and Salsipuedes. There was a set of three public phones in the shop. A metre marked how much one had spent in a call and it had to be paid to the shop owner. William decided to get off there, he made six calls, but didn't have the money to pay for them. The shop owner phoned me, and I had to go and pick him up and pay for his calls. Again, we talked about his behaviour, that if he hadn't paid the shop owner would be out of pocket, and that was like being a thief.

Every different situation had to be explained to him until he could grasp the meaning of it.

That summer, 1995, William was at home until the end of February. As usual, with William, there were ups and downs, good days, and lots of meltdowns in between.

As I had mentioned before, William liked to look at reference books, and he owned a collection of seven thin books: The Rain, The Fire, The Earth, The Air, The Water, The Solar System, The Seasons. One day, he went down the steps to the river, and along the river to the bridge. He must have dropped one of the books and he only became aware of it when he got to the bridge. According to William, and he is very amused by this story, when he got to the bridge, he met some boys and he gave them the six remaining books. When he got home, he was upset because he didn't have any of his books and I told him we would have to buy the collection again, and then he was relieved and happy. Even now, he likes to tell this story and he laughs when he asks me what happened when he got home and told me he had given his books away.

In March he went back to Granja Pia, during the week, and back home on weekends.

He related very well to a member of staff called Sonia. William liked Sonia and looked for her to do his activities with her. He tells the story that one afternoon he was with Sonia, and she wanted to go to the toilet but he would not let her go apparently, Sonia really needed to go to the toilet but William was pulling her, and Sonia hit him with a thin cane, and William let her go!

There were three boys that William liked a lot. Although he did not really relate to them, he liked to look at them and tell stories about them. Jupita, Pablo, and Gaston. According to William, every time Jupita's mother, Mirta, brought him back to Granja Pia, on a Monday, Jupita started to cry and did not want to stay. According to William, and I have no proof of this, all the staff hit Jupita with a whip and told him to behave properly. Eventually, Jupita left Granja Pia and went to live in Salta (a city in the North of Argentina). Pablo moved to Buenos Aires because his parents moved over there. Gaston stayed in Granja Pia. Although there were rumours about abusive behaviour, most parents were very happy and the boys seemed quite contented there as well. I don't really believe these rumours were true at all.

Every weekend William talked about the police building the runway, and we laughed as we talked about what police did, about thieves, and not knowing how to build runways.

On the 23rd of June 1995, there was a strike, and the Trade Union members were rioting in the streets of Cordoba. I thought it was a bit dangerous for William to take the bus into Cordoba, and I phoned Sonia to ask her not to send William that Friday on the bus, and I would pick him up in the morning the following day. Why this story is amusing to him, only William knows, but he likes this story a lot.

Apart from filming with the video camera at weekends when he was at home, William carried a mini-cassette recorder with him all the time, and he would record people talking without them noticing. He also recorded music and different sounds. Sometimes, the other boys in Granja Pia objected to being recorded, and sometimes they were jealous of him having such a "precious object". William also had a cassette player and listened to his favourite music. I must mention here that most residents in Granja Pia came from poor families, and they looked at William's possessions with envy.

On the 16th of August 1995, when William got up in the morning, he realised that somebody had taken his mini-cassette recorder. He started to shout and cry, and Olga told him she had an idea that Victor, one of the other residents, could have taken it. Victor had a physical disability but was quite clever and went to school in San Agustin. The rest of

151

the residents did not attend school. Olga and William went to Victor's school and Olga asked Victor's teacher permission to talk to him. According to William, to begin with, Victor denied having taken the mini-cassette recorder. Olga must have been quite sure of what she was doing, so, and again, according to William, Olga pulled Victor's hair and he gave her the mini-cassette recorder. This is a story that keeps coming up, and William likes to tell his current carers. Instead of telling the stories himself, William wants me to tell them to other people, and he would say: "Tell her/him when Olga pulled Victor's hair, "or, "Tell the story when I could not see Jupiter," etc. He doesn't want to tell the story himself; he would speak through me. He still does this, for example when he has done something wrong, or broken something. He might tell me part of what had happened, but he wants one of his carers to tell me the whole story. Again, he doesn't speak in third person anymore, but he wants to speak through somebody else, a spokesperson! I do think this is the unresolved issue of not assuming his own self. This is something very embedded in autistic people. I wonder if all of us, "normal people", have this issue at heart as well. Isn't it easier to let go and "free

152

ourselves" at a mascarade party, pretending to be somebody else?

According to William, on the 12th of November 1995, I went to Granja Pia with my parents to attend a big BBQ party. Olga and Alberto wanted to expand Granja Pia and they were looking at some bigger properties. Olga wanted to show me a property she really liked, and we went to visit it with my parents and William. It was near lunchtime, and William was afraid the rest of the people would eat all the food and there would not be any left for him. William started to nag, and to shout that he wanted to go back, Olga got annoyed with him and told him off. We soon went back, and we all had our lunch.

You have probably noticed by now that all the stories that William likes to tell, have some episode when somebody is annoyed, somebody gets smacked, hair pulled, somebody falling, or similar stories. I wonder if this links to William liking dangerous situations, or maybe it's his "shadenfreude" sense of humour?

One Sunday morning, William and Reggie were on their own. Reggie was reading, and William was listening to music. Reggie hadn't noticed that William had gone outside. After a little while, Reggie got a phone call from the police station to say that a policeman had spotted William running on our roof, and he thought it was dangerous. As I mentioned when I described our house, the garden sloped down, and the back of the house was three stories high. If William had fallen from the roof he could have been killed or hurt himself badly,

William likes to get into dangerous situations to see what will happen. The problem is that he doesn't take into account the consequences of his actions.

At the beginning of 1995, I stopped sharing a bedroom with Reggie and moved to the third bedroom. Our marriage was over and I just wanted to be on my own. Roderick needed a bit more privacy, especially when his friends came to sleepover. I moved William to the bedroom located off the garage. Although this bedroom was very cold, William was at home only on weekends, and I warmed it up before William went to bed.

In July we had a potential buyer for the house, who had made us a very good offer. I begged Reggie to accept it and go back to the UK, but he turned it down. I was very upset, and told Reggie that as soon as Roderick finished his high-school I would go back to England with William, and if he and Roderick wanted to come as well, they would be very welcome. Reggie did not consider that William would be better supported in the UK, but I knew that the services for people with autism would help him with the support he needed.

William came home for the summer, the day before Christmas, and we all spent Christmas at Unquillo, with the rest of our extended family.

Reggie had a school friend, Allan Watt, who lived in Amersham, north of London, with his wife Sheila. They invited Roderick to spend three months with them, during the Argentine school holidays, and attend school there. Roderick left on January 1st, 1996 and came back on the 3rd of April. This was a good experience for Roderick, a taste of school in England, and he had a good time with Allan and Sheila. It also gave him a break from the problems at home. (Roderick was 16 years old).

At the airport, Roderick off to the UK!

That summer I tried to do many activities with William. I took him once a week to Los Cocos to the chairlift, and he also tried the Superslide where he had to slide down sitting on a hessian rug. He had endless fun on both rides.

On one of the trips to Los Cocos, the subject of the policeman building the runway came up, and as usual, I asked him why he wanted a runway built, and why he wanted to come home every night. I had asked him this many times before, but as usual with William, he would not do or say anything until the time was right for him. On this occasion, he was ready to talk, and I was completely shocked and heartbroken by his answer. In his own words, he told me that Juan Carlos (an older orphan boy who had lived in Granja Pia for many years) crossed over to his bed

156

at night *"and he put his penis inside my bottom hole."* In other words, the poor soul was being raped! I was extremely sad, and annoyed with myself for not having realised that there must have been something like this behind the building of the runway. I was never able to find out how Juan Carlos was bribing or blackmailing William so that he wouldn't tell Olga or Alberto about his night escapades. I think Juan Carlos must have threatened William that had he said anything, William would have to go without lunch, or dinner. Juan Carlos was a helper in the kitchen, and William loves his food! I could not find any more details from William. I asked him if this was something that happened every night, and if it hurt him, etc, but he just repeated himself, and said nothing else. I have asked him again through the years, but he won't provide any more details. Needless to say, as soon as we got home, I phoned Olga, and she was as shocked as myself and promised to talk to Juan Carlos. Juan Carlos denied everything, but I know it is true as William never tells lies. People with autism don't tell lies, they can't understand that telling a lie could be to their benefit. For example, if William breaks something, instead of hiding it, he either tells me straight away, or admits it when I ask him. He doesn't realise that maybe he could blame somebody else or hide it under the sofa. Again, he can't see the consequences of his actions. I'm absolutely certain that Olga did not know what was going on, and I never blamed the staff for what happened to William.

Obviously, I could not send William back to Granja Pia in March. Poor William, he enjoyed Granja Pia during the day, but nights must have been a nightmare, and he kept silent for two years! I still blame myself for not realising that something was wrong for him at night. I can't even think what this must have meant to William, not only for the rapes, but because William doesn't like to be touched at all, and he must have endured it as best as he could.

I remained in contact with Olga, Alberto, and the staff, and we went to Granja Pia for BBQs and parties. William enjoyed going there with me, during the day, knowing that then we both came home.

Since then, and to date, William doesn't pronounce the name of Granja Pia when he talks about it, he only says G, prompting me to complete the name.

There was a primary school for Adults in Salsipuedes, called C.E.N.P.A. This was for adults who had not been able to go to school, either because they had developmental problems, or maybe because they came from a rural or poor family, and had to help with the parents' work, looking after younger siblings, or similar problems. The teacher, Matilde, had a very good disposition, and welcomed William into her classroom. The classes were in the evening, and William could walk there on his own.

Three times a week, in the morning, a local PE teacher took William for runs, and a bit of physical exercise. The other two mornings were spent with an educational psychologist, Mariana, in the village. Mariana was excellent and she did a lot for William but, unfortunately, she left as she had a degree in IT and got a job in Cordoba. But William went to Mariana's for a few months, remained friends with her, and visited her from time to time. To begin with, William accepted some of the tasks that Matilde gave him, but as months went by, he was just writing his calendars and was happy to be there all evening but in his own world. In other words, although Matilde gave him her best, William was not getting the stimulation he needed. At the end of the school year Matilde told me she could not have him again in 1997 as he had started to disrupt the classes. William also refused to go out again with Graciela, the PE teacher.

William's fluency, in Spanish and English, is very good. He can write in both languages without any spelling mistakes. His problem is communication. He relates to people in a bizarre way. He likes to talk to people, but his conversations seem odd to others. If William is with me, he would ask me to tell his stories to the people we meet. The main problem is that he might ask me to tell his stories while we are in a queue in the Post Office, to the person in front of us who doesn't know us at all! He likes to talk to his carers, or to people he knows, by changing the word order for them to give them the correct word order. For example:

Jeremy is having breakfast like Chubby Paddington. And we need to say: Nooo, like Chubby Checker and like London Paddington station.

Sonia is having lunch like Shirley Lomond. Nooo, like Shirley Bassey and like Loch Lomond.

And like the examples above, his imagination runs wild and can think of many combinations.

Another story that comes up in conversation, and presented to people who don't know how to answer it, is: *The plate is crying because Sonia hit him with a cane because the clock keeps changing in October.* The answer he likes to get is: The plate cannot cry because plates don't have eyes, Sonia doesn't hit anybody, and the clock will stop changing sometime in the future. And there are several combinations about the plate crying.

With his cousins, mainly when we were camping, he liked to tell them the beginning of a singer's name, for them to finish it. For example, *Fausto Pape,* and they had to say: Fausto Papetti. *Neil Dia,* they had to complete it: Neil Diamond. He laughed with this game, he called it his joke. It is an example of William's sense of humour. This "joke" has been a constant, through the years, in William's conversation.

During the summer of 1997, I went camping with William (then 18) on my own. My parents had gone to Brazil with my sister, but we could not afford to go as well. I didn't mind as I knew most of the other campers and could chat with them while William had fun in the river. We had some wild storms, and William could not go to the river on those days, but he was all right this time.

When the school year started again in March, William was registered at a school for children with special needs in Unquillo, Escuela Luis Morzone. He had to take a bus to Rio Ceballos, get off at the bus terminal, and take another bus to Unquillo. William has always liked to go on public transport, and he enjoyed the trip to school and back. William used to take a small bottle of Coca-Cola, and some biscuits to eat as a snack at school. William doesn't like to drink from a bottle, he always likes to use a glass. One day, instead of having his coke at school, he took it into the coffee shop of the bus terminal in Rio Ceballos. He took a glass from the counter and sat down to drink his coke. The owner of the coffee shop thought that William had also taken a bottle of coke, and didn't believe William. Virginia, the owner, sent me a note to go and speak with her. I went there the following day and explained that William took a bottle of coke from home every day when he went to school. I also told her about William's autism. Virginia told William he was welcome to take a glass and sit there but he had to tell her first. William kept his coke to drink at the coffee shop, and he became very attached to Virginia.

As usual, William started well at school, and he liked all the teachers. One of the teachers, Marisa, was an educational psychologist, and William started going to her house for therapy sessions once a week. Marisa lived in la Quebrada, a district of Rio Ceballos. Again, William had to take a bus to Rio Ceballos, and change there to another bus going to la Quebrada. William did well on his bus trips, and he never got lost or had any problems. He then had to walk for about ten minutes to get to Marisa's. Sometimes Marisa invited him to stay overnight on weekends. She had two sons of William's age, and they had fun with William's jokes (Fausto Pape..., the plate is crying...., etc). William liked going to Marisa's.

One day William arrived at school to find out that one of the teachers, Patricia, had had an eye problem and was going to be absent for a few days. "A few days" was not acceptable, William wanted to know the exact day Patricia was going to be back and was very upset for many days. This story about Patricia and her eye problem keeps coming up, but instead of, "William was very upset about Patricia

163

not coming to school," he swaps William for Oliver Twist, Jupita, Pablo, or the dog.

Usually, when William took the bus home, at the bus terminal in Unquillo, the bus was mostly empty, and he could sit down. One day, the bus was full and there was no seat for William. He started to shout that he wanted to sit down, and a lady gave him her seat. Unknown to William, Patricia was also in the bus, but at the other end. The following day, at school, Patricia explained to William that it was not appropriate to shout like that in the bus. That day, the bus was also full, and all the seats were taken. William went to a lady, and he whispered in her ear that he wanted her seat. He had been told not to shout, and he was not shouting. Nobody had told him it was not appropriate to ask for a seat! (I had mentioned earlier on that experiences learnt could not be applied to a new situation).

William kept going to the bakers' shops and he had become friends with the owners. Sometimes he would go and visit them at home as well. Matilde, his former teacher at C.E.N.P.A., sometimes invited William to her house. Matilde had a daughter of William's age, and she found him funny. William knew that Matilde's back door was never locked during the day. Sometimes he would walk to Matilde's even if she had not invited him. He would stay for a short while and walk back home. One day he got there and went in without knocking on the door. Matilde's daughter was ill in bed and, when she heard noises, she thought a thief had come in and hid under the bed. Then she heard William's happy noises and him opening and closing the cupboards (as it was his routine when he went into other people's homes) and came out of her hiding place. I explained to William that going into a house without knocking on the door was not appropriate and that the owners did not appreciate that, the same as he didn't like it when somebody went into his room without previously knocking on the door. This story is also retold by William, but with the usual different characters.

William was free to roam around the village. Everybody knew him, and ourselves, and I felt safe to know that had he been in any kind of problem somebody would have helped him or contacted us. One day there was a phone call from the police station to let me know that William was chasing the cars and buses at the bridge on the main road. This was a busy road and very dangerous. William had seen the stray dogs running and barking at the cars, and he was copying this behaviour. He thought this was very funny.

In February 1998, William and I went to an all-inclusive complex in La Falda, in the Lower Hills of Cordoba. This complex is called Vaquerias, and it is a lovely place, with a swimming pool, a small river, and nice places to go for walks. My parents came as well for a few days. It was not a very big complex and soon we got to know everybody, and William liked telling his stories to anybody who was prepared to listen to him. There was a group of five young teenagers who thought William's stories were very funny, and we met them every evening for a session of laughter. My sister came to spend the day with us, William was upset about something, and he pulled his shorts down and showed her his bottom. To him, this was a way of showing his displeasure! (William was 19 years old).

That summer was quite stormy, and the electricity was cut off many times causing William to become quite upset. One day, while the power was off, he disappeared, and I thought he had gone to look for the EPEC lorry. I went out to look for him and asked people in the village in case anybody had seen him. Somebody told me he had seen William going along the road to Villa Silvina. It clicked on me that he had probably gone to the top of the Water Tower, where he commanded a view of the whole village and he could locate the EPEC lorry. I drove to the Tower, and William was right at the top. We drove home and I explained to him that he could not just go away without telling me where he was going. The next time the electricity was off, he left me a note saying he had gone to the Water Tower!

William always enjoys events with some kind of drama, either people or animals dying, houses on fire, somebody falling and breaking a bone, and similar happenings.

We had an American friend who owned a big house in the outskirts of Salsipuedes. Her 25-year-old son was staying with her for a couple of months. He was standing on a tall stone fence and, instead of coming down the drive, he jumped down and broke both his ankles. He had to be in a wheelchair for a month, and William found this very funny. Schadenfreude sense of humour! :(

William was having more and more meltdowns, and we were all very upset. He was a big boy by now, not the little boy that I could restrain physically. He was very tall and strong. Since he was a little baby, William, as most autistic people, has flapped his hands, either when he is happy or when he is upset. If he is happy, he flaps his hands joining the thumb and the rest of the fingers in a rapid Crab-like pincer movement, and at the same time, he makes happy noises. If he is upset, and having a meltdown, he will flap his hands at tremendous speed, bite his tongue (sometimes quite badly), and his eyes look like they are going to pop out of their sockets.

In March William started back at Escuela Luis Morzone, in Unquillo. All these schools were really good, and designed for children with special needs who could work at their own pace and participate in a group. William needed one-to-one teaching, he could work in a group activity, but none of these schools could provide such a degree of dedication to a single student. At Escuela Luis Morzone the teachers had the best of intentions, but William was there just doing whatever he wanted to do, mostly writing his stories and making calendars. Before the school

168

winter holidays, at the beginning of July, the school headmistress told me they could not cope with William any longer. I had been expecting this as I had been getting some hints from the teachers. I was very tired of trying one school after another without getting proper results.

I had already tried all the possible schools and could not think where I was going to find a placement for William. I contacted Graciela Pollan, the PE teacher that had taken William out for runs, and she was happy to take him out again. This was just a temporary patch to a problem. Graciela started working with William three times a week, and William, reluctantly, went out. She included him in a couple of tournaments, and William, being a fast runner, did quite well. This lasted a month and he decided not to go out with Graciela any longer.

His frustrations were running wild, and I could not cope with him any longer. I contacted Olga, from Granja Pia to see if it could be possible for William to go back there, but sleep on his own, in a single room and not with the rest of the boys. All the boys slept in a single dorm, with twelve bunk beds, twenty-four boys. Olga told me William could have one of the staff's rooms, and he could even lock his door if he wanted to feel safe. I agreed to take him there on the 8th of August. When I told William, he became very upset and cried a lot. I explained to him that he would have his own room, with a lock, and he could even have his cassettes and tape recorder there. He cried and cried, and Reggie had to help me get him into the car. I felt sad to cause him so much distress, but I was at the end of my tether and could not cope any longer. It was sad to leave him there in such a state. Olga promised me she would make sure William was safe in his room.

At the weekends, William came home, and he seemed happy enough. I asked him about the sleeping arrangement and if Juan Carlos had visited him, but he said he was all right and he had the room for himself and he had locked the door at night. It was not the best of solutions, but the best one at that time. My determination to come back to Britain was even stronger.

On the 27th of August, William was due to come home, by bus, to spend the weekend with us. Olga phoned me to let me know that William had a tummy ache, that she had asked him if he wanted to be picked but he said he wanted to take the bus. When he arrived home, I noticed he was not walking properly, like bending down and holding onto his tummy. I called the paramedics who thought it could be appendicitis and suggested I took him to the hospital in Cordoba. The drive to the hospital took an hour, and I could see that William was in a lot of pain. After the doctor examined him, William was taken in for surgery. My parents came to spend an hour with me, and after that, I was just on my own while waiting for the surgeon to come out and tell me how William was. The surgery lasted five hours! William had a burst duodenal ulcer and had a lot of pus in his tummy. The surgeon had done the surgery by keyhole and had cleared the infection. William was taken to a private room, with five draining tubes sticking out of his tummy. The following day he was feeling better and did not want the tubes any longer. These tubes included a catheter, and a drip. Every day the surgeon came to assess him and to explain to him the importance of having the draining tubes. Olga came to see us, and she told me that had she known it was so serious, she would not have sent him by bus. William likes to tell this story as well, and finds it amusing. Olga also told me that during the night, before William was ill, he had got up many times to go to the toilet and he had told her he had diarrhoea. It was suggested to me that the stress of being in Granja Pia had been so unbearable that it had caused him to develop the ulcer. I felt completely devastated and guilty. Every day, while in hospital, William had periods when he was screaming that he didn't want to have the tubes any longer. After 5 nights, the doctor agreed to remove his tubes and let us go home with the promise to keep an eye on the keyholes for any sign of infection, and if so to take him back to the hospital. William recovered well and had to be in bed for another week. Little by little he recovered his strength.

I now believe I had sent William to Granja Pia more for my sake, and the rest of the family's, than for his sake. We really needed a break. This made me feel even worse, and extremely guilty. I had exposed him to his worst fears. Even if he had been promised a private bedroom, the thought of being there at night, near his abuser, was no guarantee for him.

When William was feeling back to normal, he went back to Escuela America Latina, the first school he had attended in 1988. Being there, in contact with other people, it was good for him. It was not the best solution, but it gave us a break. I could go to work without having to worry that William was roaming around the streets of Salsipuedes causing problems.

William finished his school year at Escuela America Latina.

During that summer, William went to do some work with Lorena, the daughter of one of my colleges at Academia Arguello, once a week. Lorena is about the same age as William, and a beautiful person. William loved to go and work with Lorena, and they are still friends.

The summer went by, and William (then 20) started his school year at a place in El Pueblito, the next village going north from Salsipuedes, about 3km from home. William took the bus to get there, just a short trip. This was not really a school but a home for youngsters with special needs, similar to Granja Pia. They accepted William, even though he was not going to be a boarding resident. They had some schooling with one teacher for all the boys. They also did some building as they were extending the house and the boys worked as builders. It was not the best for William, but at least he would be busy and use some of his energy.

My mind was set, and I was looking forward to 2000 when I could come back to the UK. Any placement for William was just a bonus while waiting to get back.

◇◇◇

If you ask me what is the best course of action to follow with autistic people, or the best way to go about a phobia, a meltdown, or similar behaviour, I would not be able to recommend any particular set action.

Autism is complex and what helps one person may not help others, so it is vital that each individual is supported as an individual and any interventions are adapted to their specific needs.

Autism causes the brain to have different connections to a "normal" brain resulting in perceiving the world from a different perspective. There is no cure for autism. Those parents who claim they have cured their sons or daughters are misleading and deceiving. If their children had been cured then they were not autistic, they just had some autistic behaviours due to some special circumstance or experience.

I do agree, though, that some foods or drinks could exacerbate certain behaviours, while others could help maintain calm and stress-free feelings. I've been doing quite a lot of research on the effect good gut bacteria has on stimulating the nervous system and improving the symptoms of stress and anxiety. (June 2020) It maybe early days yet, but William has started taking a probiotic supplement and I think it is making a difference in his behaviour. As I said, he has taken it for a month, so this is not a conclusion that probiotics could be the panacea for a stress-free William, it is just something I'm trying to see if it indeed helps. There is no harm in trying safe "experiments". When one is put between a rock and a hard place, I guess one is prepared to try any suggestion as long as it is safe. At least I'm all for it, and it would represent a challenge to me. If anybody had suggested to me that dipping William in the Thames would have "cured" him of his autism...believe me...I would have thrown him in first thing the following morning! I was prepared to do anything to help him as long as it was safe. Now, now I'm more realistic and try to help him by talking to him and getting him to understand the world from a different perspective, society's perspective, which is not the same as his own.

Sitting down with William and explaining, over and over, until he understands the situation, seems to work most of the time. It was easier when he was a child, it is much more difficult now. Even when he understands an action, or event, he gets so worked up in his anxiety that he doesn't seem to be able to get over it.

Social stories seem to help. When William gets fixed into one of his anxieties, the trigger, most of the time, seems to be the lack of clarity with the date or time an event or action will finish (or start). For example: when is the power going to be connected again, what time will I be picked up, when is it going to be sunny again, when are they going to show this TV program again, what time will I be able to take the bus on Saturday, etc.?

In January 2000 I came to England to find out what was available for William, and jobwise for me. I was still in contact with the National Autistic Society, and they suggested a visit to a boarding school for autistic boys in Alverstoke, Gosport. I spoke to the Headmaster, Mr. Ron Clark, who thought William could fit in well, but he needed to assess him first. He showed me the premises, and it looked like a good place for William. The fact that the school had been accredited by the Autistic Society gave me the peace of mind that it was completely dedicated to supporting autistic people, and that they would be receiving the best treatment available.

While I was away, I had arranged for William to spend some time at Lorena's house, some time at home, and a few days at school. While William was at ISIM (his school), Tata, the owner, hit William with a tin on his forehead, and William had a big bruise. Lorena saw William the day after and she was shocked at his bruise. On my return, when I confronted Tata, he said he had the tin in his hand, William opened the door and was hit by accident. William told me Tata hit him because he was shouting. I tend to believe William. He never tells lies. However, William doesn't hold grudges, and remembers Tata with affection. I could not prove if it had been an accident or deliberate, maybe a bit of both.

I went back home to Rio Ceballos and started planning my move to the UK. Roderick had moved into a small flat with a friend, and had started University, studying Business Administration.

When I lived in Saline, and in Tavistock, I had a Resident's Permit, but not British citizenship. The immigration law was different then, and to become British one had to be resident in the country for 7 years without breaking that period for more than three months each time. I had been away for much longer. My mother had Italian Citizenship, and I applied for mine as well, and got it. Being Italian allowed me to come into the UK under EU law.

I felt bad about leaving Roderick on his own but had given him the choice and he had chosen to remain in Argentina. Even if it was his choice, I knew I was going to miss him dearly.

Reggie was sure that he wanted to remain in Argentina, and we thought the best way was to get divorced. We had a very simple and friendly divorce, and even used the same solicitor. He would give me thirty thousand pounds, and I would be financially responsible for our two sons. I agreed to everything as there was no point in arguing and we both wanted to sort out things for the future. I think that it does a lot of harm to the family to stay in a bad relationship. Reggie and I could not agree on anything to do with William, and we just argued too much on how to deal with him.

Before finishing this chapter, I want to add here some thoughts from Roderick:

I can't really remember much of my childhood with William. I assume that during the early years it was probably life as normal, as with any two brothers, fighting for toys, attention, etc.

However, as the years went by, the two lives started to diverge.

My clearer memories are from when we moved to Salsipuedes, Argentina, in 1988. I was going to the local school, inviting friends over, learning to ride a bike, playing football with my neighbours. Those things never happened with William. When I compared myself with other kids, William was obviously missing out on all those things, but I was also missing out on having a normal brother, with friends, arguing, fighting, etc.

I saw all my friends and cousins who would play with their brothers, their brother's friends, etc. and I think, looking back now, it's something I would have liked, that sense of having a real friend in your brother, someone in whom you can trust and grow up together.

And even as a grown-up, it would have been nice to be able to share things with my brother – going on holiday together, sharing day to day life. I recently made a trip with three of my cousins (all brothers) and we went cycling through the mountains. That sense of camaraderie, it's something that neither William nor I will be able to share. Not in the good times or the bad times.

William enjoys his life in his own way. In a certain sense, he's sociable with whoever he wants and on his own terms. I remember when I was about 17 years old, most people in our village didn't even know me (or my name) but they all knew William.

I don't think I ever felt embarrassed about having an autistic brother, there isn't really anything to be ashamed of, it's more a case of being sad of not being able to share much (or anything at all) with him. It's obviously not his fault, nor anybody's fault, for that matter.

I guess I have come to terms with having the brother I have, unfortunately, in practical terms, it's like being an only son.

Sad but true.

Chapter Five

England

William was 21 years old on Feb 11th, 2000.

On March 20th, 2000, William and I took the flight to London Heathrow.

Through a friend, I had made arrangements to rent a flat for us in Gosport. The flat was at the corner of the High Street, and it was very cosy and comfortable.

Before we came, when I told William about our trip, he was not happy at all, and I had had to reassure him that it was only for a short time.

I made an appointment to go and see Mr Ron Clark, and William had an assessment over two days. It turned out that it was not suitable for William as the other boys were far more impaired by their autism, and this would be to William's detriment.

While he was being assessed, William kept saying he did not want to be in England for longer than a month. Ron Clark told William he had to try at least for a year before saying he didn't like it here. William was very upset about this and kept saying: "I'm upset because Ron Clark told me a year". This story comes up every so often and now that he is happy here, he finds it very amusing. But back then it upset him a lot. I felt very sorry for William as I knew he was unhappy and he had not liked the change. Funnily enough, he had always accepted our international moves and changing houses. I think he didn't like the climate and he missed the freedom he had in our village.

Ron Clark suggested that the best way to go about it was to get in touch with Social Services, they would allocate William a social worker who would sort out a placement for him. And that was what I did. We had many appointments with William's new social worker, Jenny L., and we concluded that William would benefit from a placement in a home for autistic young men. These homes are shared houses, where 4 or 5 young men live together, and are well looked after 24/7 by carers.

William was not happy to be in England, and he missed Salsipuedes, his freedom to roam around the village, the weather, and, I guess, the people in his life. I'm very proud of William because it was hard for him to endure such a big change once more. Despite all the problems, he finally settled in pretty well. It was very hard on me as well. I love the UK, and I'm very happy to live here, but I had also left my other son, my parents, extended family and friends, to start all over again from scratch.

Barbra Streisand
521 Fifth Avenue
New York
NY 10017
USA
9th of June 2000
Dear Barbra:
On the 23rd of June I'm going to take the plane to the States and on the 24th of June I'm going to arrive at the airport in New York and you have to wait for me at the airport in New York and every day you have to teach me to cook and also you have to teach me to wash my clothes and also you have to teach me the money so I'm going to stay with you for one year in New York and on the 30th of June 2001 I'm going to take the plane to Argentina
Love
William Elliott
3 Crown Mews
Clarence Road
Gosport PO12 7HD
England

This letter shows how unhappy he was, and also how he likes to "escape" to other places until the situation resolves, but in the end, he was going to fly to Argentina

I wanted to make William happy and, to show him there were some advantages to living here, I decided to take

183

William to Euro Disney in Paris for a weekend. We went with a local tour company, by coach, by train under the channel, and by coach to Paris. William thoroughly enjoyed all the rides, the rougher the better. William loves roller coasters and rough rides.

◇◇◇

William started having outreach support, and an excellent carer, Hanna, came twice a week to take him out for a couple of hours.

Jenny, the social worker, suggested that William could go into a transitory home, in Fareham (4 miles from Gosport), until a proper and final placement could be found. William moved into Croft House, in Fareham. This home was managed by Social Services, and, although they catered for mixed disabilities, the carers had been trained to look after autistic people. William was very distressed, not because of Croft House, but because he had been told, by Ron Clarke, he had to be in England for at least a year.

William has always had an excellent sense of orientation, and he pays attention to detail when he walks to a place, or goes somewhere by any means of transport. Everywhere here was new to him, and he took some time to find his bearings. One day he absconded from Croft House and wanted to reach Gosport and my flat. He got completely lost and was lost for 5 hours. The staff contacted the police, and thanks to the street cameras they found William somewhere in Fareham.

Next time I picked William up and drove to Gosport, he watched for landmarks and how to get there. He absconded a second time and he succeeded in getting to the flat. I took him back and he was more settled this time. He was not unhappy at Croft House, and he liked the carers and the other residents. One of the residents, called Richard, was in a wheelchair, had many physical disabilities, and his legs were twisted. William told me that Richard had been born "horrible", and he wanted Richard to have an operation to untwist his legs.

I visited William every week, and he was settling in well in Croft House. We went for walks, to have something to eat, or for drives in the car.

I had the chance of getting a small mortgage and bought a Studio Flat in Gosport. So, I moved from Crown Mews to Holland House.

When William moved to Croft House, I got a job in Morrisons supermarket. It was not my ideal kind of job, but it was just across the street from Crown Mews and I only worked there for four hours a day. After three months I went to work at Haslar Hospital, a military hospital in Gosport. I worked in the laboratory office registering all the data. I loved the job, and the camaraderie amongst the people in the forces.

I started going out with Nigel, a friend I had met through the Butterfly Association, and he came to live with me at the end of November.

Nigel is a butterfly breeding expert, considered internationally a butterfly guru, who has written many papers and manuals on how to breed butterflies. I have translated all this into Spanish. He has got an extraordinary memory for names of plants and butterflies.

◇◇◇

At the end of 2000, just before Christmas, Roderick decided he was going to come and live in England. This made me and William very happy. Roderick got organised pretty quickly, got a job in the Ferries going to Spain and France, and after a few months moved to London. My cousin Patty lived in London and she was a big support for Roderick. Roderick got a job and went to University. He graduated with a first, in Financial Economics, and started his career with JPMorgan.

William started some courses designed for people with special needs at the local college. He was going to computer and independent skills classes. Every Thursday he was going to the local library, and sometimes he liked to borrow a CD or a DVD.

Nigel and I took him a few times to the Southampton Diving Pool, and again he was jumping down from the 10-metre diving board. One day we arrived at the Sports Centre, there had been a chlorine problem and the diving pool was closed. Two months went past, and we took him back to the pool. When we arrived, we told the receptionist that we had been there some time ago when the pool was closed. She told us William could go in for free for the trouble we had had that day, but she needed to know the exact date of our trip. William came up with the date straight away, just out of his mind! The receptionist looked it up on her computer and was very impressed!

William wanted to go and visit Tavistock again. Nigel and I organised the trip and picked William up early one morning. It is a five-hour drive from Gosport to Tavistock. We arrived there about lunch time, and headed to The Harvest Inn, the pub we used to go to as a family when we lived there. We went to see Gulworthy School, but found that the school was no longer there, and a Camping and Caravan Site had been established there. We also went to see our former house on Rocky Hill, and had a walk in the park. After all that was done, William said he wanted to go back to Croft House. We had planned to stay there overnight, but William was adamant that he wanted to go back and no way he wanted to spend the night there. So back we went, another 5- hour drive. Nigel and I were exhausted at the end of the day!

I was in contact with Reggie quite frequently, and he kept saying he was all right. In June 2001, I had a call from a friend, Jorge Maldonado, to tell me that he had visited Reggie, thought he had lost too much weight, and insisted on taking him to the hospital for a check-up. All sorts of tests were done, and Reggie was diagnosed with terminal cancer

188

of the colon, as a primary, but the cancer had spread to the liver and other organs. Roderick and I went to Argentina to pick up Reggie so that he could come over here to have his treatment at a hospital in England. Jorge was very helpful. It was not just bringing Reggie over, but the house and its contents had to be sold, some items had to be packed to be sent to England, and a lifetime had to be wrapped up and closed down. Jorge had a buyer for the house, and everything got sorted out in a week. I came back with Reggie, and Roderick stayed over another week to sign all the paperwork.

By moving furniture, and picking up heavy things, I had developed an inguinal hernia. Reggie was very weak, and the flight was long, which made him feel quite ill. Before flying out to Argentina, I had already spoken to my GP, and he had contacted the hospital. We arrived on a Monday, Reggie started his chemo on Wednesday, and I went into the hospital on Friday to have my hernia repair surgery. On Sunday I went back home. Reggie moved into Holland House and I went there every day to look after him and to drive him to hospital for treatment.

William was able to see Reggie from time to time, and was upset that Reggie had to sell the house. William was not aware or did not care that Reggie was so ill. He was more interested in the selling of the house. One of my cousins from Argentina, who had British nationality, had moved into Gosport with his wife. It was then very convenient (although this was a white lie) to explain to William that Reggie and Michael had to move to the UK because the Argentine government had cancelled the visas to British people due to the Falklands War. And as there were not issuing any more visas, William could not go and live in Argentina in the meantime. I know I lied to him, but sometimes it is the only way to get him to accept something. He didn't like it at all, but eventually, he accepted it.

Reggie's health deteriorated very rapidly and was in and out of the hospital, more in than out. Roderick and I were with Reggie most of the time. We knew he was not going to last long and wanted to be with him. Reggie passed away on September 8th, 2001. It was very sad, and Roderick was inconsolable. Reggie was not religious and we organised a humanitarian funeral service. Roderick spoke about his dad and made us all cry. Despite all our problems, I still considered Reggie as a great guy!

I did not want to take William to the funeral service as Reggie was going to be cremated. However, I thought William needed to have closure. I talked to the funeral parlour staff, and they prepared the open coffin for viewing. Reggie's body was covered up to his waist with a red velvet cloth. William, and his fascination with death, wanted to make sure Reggie was dead, so he picked up his arm and let it go, and then did the same with his head and his legs. I wasn't sure if I wanted to cry or to laugh. Once William was convinced Reggie was dead, he was ready to go home. He didn't appear to be sad at all. As usual, William had it all sorted out, and he said he would see his dad in 2003 when he, himself, went to heaven. From then on, he started fixing the year when he was going to pass away, in this case, 2003, but as 2001 finished he passed 2003 to 2004....and he is still at it. At the moment, he is going to pass away in 2023, but at the end of this year, he will transfer it to 2024. For a few years, when he was not sure if he wanted to live here or in Argentina, he said he was going to be reborn in Argentina! Clever boy, being born in Argentina meant having

Argentinian nationality, and he didn't need a visa any longer!

I feel very sorry for Reggie as he never saw the end of the "Plan de Convertibilidad", when the dollar and the Argentine Peso were 1 to 1. It was at the end of 2001 when the economic crisis exploded and they had to scrap the 1 to 1, but Reggie had already passed away.

◇◇◇

I changed my job and started working for Social Services as a home carer, and then I became a team leader for the Out of Hours Department. I really enjoyed my work with Hampshire County Council Social Services. It was a very rewarding job and I thoroughly recommend it.

William was in Croft House for two years. There were some possible services where he could have moved into but were not suitable for many reasons. There was a home in Eastbourne, but it was over 80 miles from Gosport, too far away for me to visit William. They were waiting for a home that was going to be opened in New Milton, Hampshire, about an hours-drive from Gosport. Finally, on February 12th, 2002, William moved into Rose House, together with another 4 young men. William was allocated a big bedroom

192

overlooking the road. Rose House was a big house, with a garden at the back, and about a mile from New Milton town centre. William seemed to be much more settled, and happy to be in England. William was 23 years old then.

While William was in Croft House, he had two outreach carers that worked with him several times a week. These two carers became part of the permanent staff in Rose House, and it was a way of having continuity for William. I was very grateful for the way things had been organised, and this made the transition, from Croft House to Rose House, much easier for William.

William appeared to be happy in New Milton. The carers were great with William, and he accepted to do all sorts of activities. He joined some classes at Brockenhurst College and even went sailing during the warmer months. Sailing classes were provided by the Special Needs Unit of the college, and they took place in a local lake.

I won't mention here all of William's review for 2002, but only what I consider relevant. These reviews were written by the carers, I have added my comments in italics:

- That William had good self-care skills but sometimes needed prompting. William was very good at getting up and having a shower, brushing his teeth, and all his ablutions, but got distracted and needed prompting.

- When anxious he displayed certain behaviours like shouting, swearing, kicking, headbutting, or trying to run across the road. Triggers for this behaviour: other residents entering his room, or to get a desired response to a specific request that it was impossible to meet. *William's patience is not one of his virtues and he can't understand why his requests are not met.*

- Calming Techniques: Reassure William. Redirect him onto another activity. Remind him his actions are unacceptable. Allow him time to calm down in his room. Spend time with him to discover the source of his anxiety, but only after he has calmed down.

- William couldn't comprehend the value of money and cannot budget.

- William went to college for independent skills, and to do a computer course.

- William enjoyed physical activities like walking and swimming. He liked going to the charity shops to buy old LP records. *William loves his LP records and has a great collection of different types of music.*

I started taking William out on the train. I drove to New Milton, picked William up, left the car at the railway station, and we went to different cities, mostly Winchester, Bournemouth, or Southampton. William loved the train trips, and he also started going out by train with his carers. William loves all kinds of public transport, but the railway is his favourite. I visited William every three weeks and phoned him every day. William did not want me to stay in his house for any length of time. I had to pick him up and go, he did not want me to speak to his carers or to the manager. He didn't want to come to our house either and this suited me well. William used to pace back and forth, he could have had a meltdown at any time, and I was not sure how Nigel would have dealt with this.

Twice a year, the manager organised a trip to one of the Theme Parks near Southampton, and the five residents went together with a few carers. William really enjoyed these trips. I also took him, several times, to Butlin's in Bognor Regis, and to Alton Towers in Stoke-on-Trent.

William wanted to go back to Edinburgh, and to the Marriott Hotel, where he had to be dragged out and the manager had filmed him screaming that he wanted to stay in the hotel (in 1986).

We went there by train in June 2003. As soon as we went into the Marriott Hotel William noticed they had changed the carpets that used to be blue back in 1986. As I mentioned before, William has an eye for detail. We stayed there for two nights, then took the train to Carlisle, stayed there for a night, and went to Alton Towers for another two nights. It was very exhausting for me, but William was happy and behaved well. I made this trip for many years, and 4 years ago I decided it was too much for me to spend so many days with William all on my own, and decided to make two, or more, shorter trips along the year.

I haven't got William's review for 2003, but by 2004 William had improved in certain things and his review stated the following:

- William displays self-care skills with only a little prompting. He has a routine that he follows and helps him not to get distracted.

- William can dress himself but needs prompting to dress according to the weather. William doesn't suffer the cold or the heat as "normal" people do, and he finds it very difficult to choose appropriate clothes for the current weather.

- William is a private person who finds it difficult to forge relationships with his peers. *William relates well to his carers but not to his peers whom he tends to ignore.*

- William enjoys going to College, although he gets distracted in class with his own thoughts.

- William likes watching videos of different countries. William borrows these videos from the library.

- William enjoys going to the railway station to watch the trains and to listen to the announcements. *He knows most of the announcements by heart.*

- William needs to develop social skills in the community. At the moment, William stands too close, without any regard to other people's personal space. He will also say inappropriate things, or will touch people he hardly knows, usually on the arm.

- Problem Behaviour: When anxious he could damage fixtures and fittings in the house. Screaming, swearing, biting his tongue, kicking doors. Triggers: Being told at the library that they didn't have the video requested by him. Other residents becoming anxious. Other residents going into his room. Losing or misplacing a personal item. Calming Techniques: Calm and reassure tone of voice. Time to calm down listening to music in his room. Redirection when possible. Reassuring him that staff are available to listen to him and help him. Offering to hold his hands. Breathing technique to calm him down.

- During the last two years William has talked a lot about going back to Argentina, about dying and being born there, but now he seems happy here, and only talks about visiting Argentina in the future.

- William can become very animated on subjects that interest him. He enjoys storytelling, and roll playing his stories. But if you ask him a question that he is not interested in, he will tell you "I don't know" or "it is a "secret".

- William has an obsession with the postal system, and he waits every morning for the postman to arrive. He becomes anxious if the post is late, or if his letters are not returned. Reassure William that sometimes the post will be late but will eventually come.

- Asking the same question over and over. It helps to write it down, and to redirect him to his notebook when he asks again the same question.

- Asking the full name, and often the address, and country of origin, of staff at the supermarket, or restaurants. Remind William that people may not wish to tell him his personal details. Saying "it is private" often helps.

I must add here, as some advice for parents of autistic children, that it is very important to have a Care Plan, with input from your child. It will give you focus, objectives and aims, and you will be able to match it with the progress your son or daughter is achieving.

In 2004, when William was 25, Roderick moved to Argentina and got married to Analia Guell, his childhood friend. He got transferred from London JPMorgan to the branch in Buenos Aires. Rod and Analia lived in

Salsipuedes, Rod worked in Buenos Aires during the week and flew home at weekends.

On February 2nd, 2005, Nigel and I got married at Fareham Registrar Office. We had a very small party with only twelve guests.

In September 2005 Jeremy was born, and I went in October to meet my grandson.

In January 2006 I took William to Argentina (William age 27). The flight itinerary was London/ Barcelona/ Madrid/ Santiago de Chile/ Córdoba. It was a combined flight British Airways/ Iberia. The flight from London was on time, but the one from Barcelona was delayed due to a technical problem, and we missed the connection at Madrid. The airline provided accommodation at the airport hotel as the next flight was at 10pm the following day. William loved it. From our hotel window, William had a complete view of the runway and he could see the planes landing and taking off. He was fascinated by this, and since then he has always asked to be taken to the local airport to watch the planes. The flight from Madrid was also delayed for technical problems and we missed the connection at Santiago de Chile, and we spent another night at the airport hotel. William could not believe his luck. We finally arrived in Cordoba after three days' travelling. We had twelve days in total, and we had spent three days travelling. We stayed with my parents in a self-catering bungalow in Salsipuedes, and William was happy to visit all the shop owners. We visited Roderick, Analia, and Jeremy, and William stayed there for two nights.

William spent a night at Lorena's house as well and had a fantastic time there. Marisa, his former teacher and educational psychologist, had moved from la Quebrada to a town, up north in the Province of Cordoba, called Capilla del Monte. William had sent Marisa an email to let her know he would be in Cordoba. Marisa phoned me and invited William to go to Capilla del Monte, and she promised to phone me that Friday to arrange the time she would pick William up. Friday came, the weekend went past, but Marisa never phoned me. William was very upset and disappointed, and I could not understand why Marisa never let us know that she was not able to have William over. Had she explained to William that something had turned up and she could not have him over, William would have been upset but he would have understood.

The flight back was uneventful, and William behaved really well.

Back home, William kept on talking about how sad he was that Marisa had not contacted him, and that he could not understand why she had not phoned him. As I have mentioned it before, drastic events, or explanations, work well with William. Soon after that, I told William that Marisa's husband had sent me an email to let me know that Marisa was coming back from Brazil, by coach, and it turned over several times and ended up at the bottom of a cliff and Marisa had died instantly. That did it for William. He said: "I'm going to be sad only for today because I am going to see Marisa when I go to heaven in 2007". That was it, problem sorted.

My cousins find this very amusing and told me I have become a phantom killer. First, I "killed" the guy who was going to build the runway, then Marisa, and I will tell you later about some more of my "phantom victims"!

It was around this time that I could see that William, apart from calculating the day of the week of any set date, and making long mathematical calculations, could also tell the time in different countries located in different time

202

zones. He used to, and still does, ask me if a plane takes off at a certain time from an X airport, at what time does it arrive at Y airport. I need to look at my mobile phone to give him the correct answer, but he provides me with the answer before I have time to open the app. William expects me to remember the answer, and loves to trip me up!

William has kept writing in his notebooks, either calendars, or stories. Most of the stories he writes are the ones I have been recalling here, and only the main character changes.

Sometimes, if he is waiting for something to end, or if he doesn't like a situation, he says he is going to stay in a castle until the end of the situation. It could change from a castle, to jail, to a flat in Scotland, to a house in Argentina, etc. William has never liked it when the clock changes in October, but he doesn't mind when it changes in March. For some obscure reason, he likes it when there is a 4-hour difference between here (UK) and Argentina. When it changes in October there is a 3-hour difference, and he hates it. He starts getting anxious at the beginning of September, and sometimes he said he would like to be in a castle until the clock changed back again. The conversation went like this: "I would like to be in a castle until the clock changes again", William told me on the phone.

My answer was: "William, you won't like it, castles are cold and there won't be anybody to look after you in a castle."

"But I want to be in a castle and one of my carers could come and look after me."

"Ok", I replied, "ask Christine (the manager) to organise it for you."

"What is Christine going to tell me?" William asked me.

"I don't know, William, I'm not Christine."

"But I want to know what she is going to tell me," replied William.

"I think she will tell you that you live in your house and you should stay there, otherwise everybody will miss you," I said.

"OK, I'm not going to go to a castle," William concluded, and that is the end of the conversation.

Sometimes, if the place he wants to go is jail, he knows he would need to have done something bad to go to jail, and he says: "I'm going to grab an old lady's handbag in the street so a policeman can take me to jail".

As I have mentioned it before, William used to go to visit Matilde, in Salsipuedes. He always wanted Matilde to invite him to sleep over, but Matilde kept saying she didn't have a spare bed for William. Very understandable, and I don't blame her for that. William always talks, even now, about Matilde building a spare bedroom so he can go and stay overnight. But as usual, he has it all sorted out. He has developed a story where either Jupita, Gaston, or Pablo (the boys from Granja Pia), go to the USA, to stay over with different singers. He has worked it out where these singers live: Bob Dylan in San Francisco, John Denver in Colorado, Kenny Rogers, the relatives of Burl Ives in Seattle (B.I, J.D and K.R are dead so it is their relatives he is going to visit), and other singers in different cities. So, whoever the character is at that moment, takes the plane from Cordoba to Buenos Aires, and from there to Miami, but the plane from Cordoba has a puncture, and leaves two hours late, the plane from Buenos Aires has a problem with the starter and leaves two hours late, and by the time he arrives in Miami, the connected flight (to wherever he was going) had left, and he has to stay in a hotel overnight. Finally, the plane from Miami to the selected city leaves and he arrives at the airport, and takes a taxi to the singer's house. When he arrives, he tells the singer that he has come to stay because he is a bit sad because Matilde hasn't got the room ready, and the singer invites him in. Every day he phones Matilde until one day Matilde tells him the room is ready. He then tells the singer that he is going back as the room is ready. He takes a taxi to the airport, boards the plane to Miami, flies to Buenos Aires, then to Cordoba, his mother is waiting at the airport and drives him to Matilde's house. But after spending the night there, he doesn't behave very well. He either puts his fingers in the vacuum cleaners brush and cuts his fingers, or he breaks the TV, or he kicks the door of the wardrobe, or similar behaviour. This is a very long story, and it requires the timing of the flights, the delays, different time zones, and detailed planning. Although the characters change, it is always William with a different identity!

◇◇◇

In June we went again to the Marriott Hotel in Edinburgh. William went up and down the stairs a million times, we also spent time in the swimming pool, and in the jacuzzi. We took the bus into town, walked to the castle, along Princess St, and had a meal at a restaurant. The following day we went to Saline, and the new owners of our former house let us in. We had a great time looking around and walking in the garden. From there we went to Dunfermline to visit Peggy Rutherford. Peggy had moved into a flat when her children got married and left home. On that trip we did not go to Alton Towers, but later on, in September I took William to Butlins.

William's review for 2006 said:

- William doesn't need any prompting with self-care. As time went by William learnt to deal with his self-care without any prompting.

- William enjoys going to college, and his concentration in class has improved. His interaction with the staff, and other students, has increased.

- William enjoys contact with the assistants he meets in local shops.

- William enjoys walks to the beach, and going to Water Parks

- William enjoys wordplay with staff members. He also likes telling them something in Spanish for them to beg him to translate what he had said.

- Triggers for challenging behaviour: similar to last year plus: His computer not working and being unable to send an email. if a CD or DVD he has ordered over the internet has not arrived within the expected time. Calming Techniques: same as last year.

- Sometimes William likes mimicking challenging behaviour displayed by other residents. He then needs to be reminded that it is not acceptable.

- William is more at ease at college with staff and students, and he participates when required.

- William could be intolerant of other people's needs, interrupting conversations, and demanding attention.

- William is bilingual in English and Spanish, and sometimes tries to teach the staff some words in

Spanish. *William can read and write in both languages without any spelling mistakes.*

- When William is happy, he is constantly on the move, jumping up and down, talking to himself, and flapping his hands.

- Although William can accept changes, with ample warning, he functions best when following a planner or rota. As long as one explains to William that a time or activity needs to be changed, he seems to accept this without too much trouble.

- William continues to have a one to one support in the community.

I must add here that William (aged 27) had made a lot of progress and was able to function better in the community. Being looked after by carers who understood autism made an incredible difference in his behaviour. Sometimes us, parents, think that is better to keep our children at home instead that in a "home" looked after by carers. I'm convinced that when they become adults, they need their independence from us, and properly trained staff are a real plus.

On December 8th, 2006, my mother was going to be 80 years old and she was planning a big party. I had already bought my ticket and was getting ready to fly to Argentina, for two weeks, on the 6th. At the end of November, I was in the office when I got a call from Nigel to say he had been passing blood in his urine all day. I went home and took him to the hospital. He had a scan and was diagnosed with kidney cancer. We were sent to see a consultant, and to have a CT Scan. The consultant told us that the cancer was encapsulated inside the kidney and that the surgery had been planned for January the 6th. Nigel said, and I quote, "Nothing you can do, don't change your plans, just go to Argentina and enjoy your mum's birthday party."

I went to Argentina, but in a sombre mood, and tried to enjoy my mother's birthday and the company of relatives and friends.

Nigel had his surgery, there was no chemo needed, and after many months he recovered completely. His tumour was a T4 (terminal), and the surgeon told him he could live two more years, but he could be lucky and live for much longer.

In November 2007, Nigel and I went to Argentina for a month. We had already been there a few times, and Nigel loved the place. I haven't mentioned this before, but Nigel lived in Malawi, and in Sudan, for 10 years, when he was working for the British government mapping the world. He loved his years over there, the butterflies were amazing, he even found two new unknown species, and he learnt how to speak a local dialect in Malawi, and Arabic in Sudan.

While we were in Rio Ceballos Nigel told me that he would love to move to Argentina, that if he had only a few years to live he would rather live them in a place with lots of sunshine. This was a great dilemma for me. On the one hand, I knew William was going to be very sad, on the other hand, I had to consider Nigel, my parents (who were getting on in years), and the fact that my only grandson lived in Salsipuedes, and also my other son, Roderick.

During that trip, we stayed in Rio Ceballos, in a house that my cousin Patty, and her husband (also called Nigel), (living in the UK) had purchased online to move over there the following February. Patty and I are very close friends, and my Nigel and her Nigel are great butterfly friends. They encouraged us to move to Argentina, both Nigels could go out collecting together, and we could have a great time. We looked at several properties and made up our mind to move over there. We had to sell the flat and our house in the UK. We came back and put the flat up for sale and, in no time, we had a buyer. I went back to Argentina, on my own, to look at more properties, and bought a house with two acres of ground. The house was not very big, but there was scope to extend it. It was a good investment as it was less than half the price of other properties we had seen, and we could then extend it based on our own project.

When I told William we were going to move to Argentina, he took it really well, but, of course, William tends to react later on, when he processes the information. We moved there at the beginning of October, and I had arranged for William to go and visit us in December.

Chapter Six

Argentina versus England

William's behaviour seemed to be calm and settled. He was 28 years old.

Some good friends, who knew William quite well were travelling to Argentina to see their family and they were quite happy to support William during the flight. I'm very grateful to Gaby Heinz and her husband Dave for accompanying him to Argentina and back. I must also mention here that before Gaby got married to Dave she lived in Brighton and William went to visit her many times and even spent the night at her house. He has a great affection for Gaby, and even now, in 2020 he always talks about her, and is in contact with her by email. Gaby, Dave and their three daughters moved to Australia many years ago. William keeps saying he would like Gaby to move back to the UK.

The three of them flew over on December 8th, 2008, and the return flight was in January, 2009. William stayed with us for a month.

When we had just arrived at our new house, in Rio Ceballos, we had borrowed a few items of furniture, and we had some basic cooking utensils to get by, for some time until our container arrived. The container was not due to arrive until sometime in January.

We had contracted Ruben, our builder, to start the extension. He was well known by my family, and I could trust him to do things properly. He started building the double garage the day after our arrival. The project was to build a double garage, workshop, and pantry, with a total of seventy-four square metres. This was supposed to be completed by the time the container arrived so that we could put all the boxes and furniture there and start bringing things little by little into the house.

The rest of the project consisted of a guest house (72sq metres), a "quincho" (entertainment area with big BBQ, kitchen, bathroom and a small bedroom, 72sq metres), and a swimming pool.

For some unknown reason, the container was sent earlier than planned, and it arrived at the end of November. We had all the boxes and furniture inside the main house.

We couldn't start organising ourselves because the electrician was rewiring the whole house.

When William arrived, we could not offer him a proper space for himself, and he became a bit anxious. Every day I took him to a nearby Lido, and that made him happy. We also visited all his "friends" and went for daily trips into the mountains.

William wanted me for himself, he was jealous of Nigel, and he picked some small quarrels which provoked meltdowns. William was not only jealous of Nigel, but of anybody else who came to visit us.

William left with Gaby and Dave, and he was good on the return trip.

We had agreed that I would phone William every night, and that he would send me a maximum of three emails every day. Had this maximum not been agreed, William's obsessions could have resulted in fifty emails a day. He could have said everything in one mail, but his emails have different subjects and for him, it is important to separate them into three different ones. I had also agreed to come to England every June and stay for a month to take William out every day. It is very important to set

215

boundaries, this helps William to feel more settled and to know what to expect.

For some time, William continued to be settled and happy, and well supported by his carers.

I travelled to England in June 2008 and stayed at a B&B just up the road from Rose House. We went to Edinburgh, and to Alton Towers for a total of 5 days. We also went out on the train to many places nearby, and to London. William behaved well and was happy. I was sad to leave him and felt guilty as well. William did not have any other relatives in England, and only had his carers to take him out. He could see that the other residents were picked up by their parents, but he had nobody to do so for him.

When Christmas arrived, the other residents went home, and William spent Christmas on his own with a carer. William started developing some anxieties, and he started to break some of his things, like self-harming. He started with his computer mouse, and in a few months, he had broken thirty of them. He also broke keyboards, screens, DVD players, CD players, and other things.

I couldn't find anybody to take him to Argentina for a visit, and, anyway, it would have been difficult to cope with William and Nigel together. When I was visiting him in June, he could not tolerate anybody else with us, he wanted to monopolise my time.

So, a whole year went past, and I saw William again in June 2009. I knew he was very well looked after, but I was worried about his anxieties and his self-harming.

William started to speak even more about dying young and being born again in Argentina. He started saying he wanted to smoke cigarettes so he could get lung cancer, die, and be born again. He also wanted to put his fingers in the socket so he could get electrocuted.

This was written by one of his carers:

William has demonstrated episodes of behaviour which have given cause for concern. There appeared to have been a series of incidents, of different behaviours, which can be categorised as attempts to self-harm and damage property. These include superficial cuts to his fingers, swallowing a piece of metal which led to a hospital visit and Xray, climbing on furniture to lean off of his bedroom

217

window, causing damage to his own property, and periods of screaming.

But I was sure that William did not have suicidal thoughts, he just wanted to see what happened and it was also part of his "contradictory syndrome", and the more I told him not to do it the more he would do it. All this made me feel very sad for William.

In May, my mother was diagnosed with terminal pancreatic cancer, and I was grateful to be able to look after her. She passed away on August 26th. Although I was sad, and guilty for being away from William, I was grateful to be able to be with my dad at such an unhappy time. My sister and I talked my father into moving closer to us in Rio Ceballos, and he sold his house and moved into a nice house in the town, about 2.5 km from us. I was glad to be there to comfort my dad, who was eighty-six by then.

Not long after William moved into Rose House, he started having great pleasure in sending letters to different addresses in different countries that he looked up on the internet. He is still doing this now in 2020. He sends them to the correct address but addresses them to famous people.

He does that in order to get them returned to him. Sometimes he addresses the letters to famous people, and sometimes he sends them to funny made-up names, like "Shirley Cigarette". He sends letters to different countries, Russia, India, Madagascar, South Africa, Costa Rica, etc, and he gets most of them back. I'm grateful for the people who take the trouble to write: "not known at this address" and post them back. William has a big box full of these letters. Sometimes he tells me he has not received such and such a letter, and I tell him that probably those people live far away from a Post Office.

William has also written to several fan-clubs of some of his favourite singers and got some kind of certificate back saying he is part of the fan Club.

William continued breaking his things, and I agreed with the staff to make him wait some time to replace the broken item. William waited patiently, got the replacement and broke it again. He also started touching people in the train, on the sleeve or the arm. William was told this was not appropriate and that he, himself, didn't like to be touched, so not to touch other people. All this made me feel very guilty as I knew he was missing me and felt he had nobody else apart from his carers. The carers were very patient with him and produced social stories to help him understand his own feelings.

I kept visiting William every year in June, and we took our yearly trip to Edinburgh. William wanted to spend some time at the airport watching the planes land and take off, listening to the announcements, and watching the flight information boards. Sometimes he wanted to touch the boards and he was told off. In one of these visits, he started going UP the escalator on the DOWN escalator. He tried it several times. I was trying to prevent him from doing it, and finally, the security guard told us to leave the airport unless we were taking a flight. We left and went back to the hotel.

◇◇◇

William behaved quite well on our daily trips on the train to his favourite cities. The trips always go like this, we take the train and arrive at his choice of city, we walk to the restaurant he has chosen (usually Burger King, McDonald's, or any of the Weatherspoons pubs), eat our meal (William will always have lasagna or some other pasta at the pub, and the usual burger and chips in the other venues), I will draw all his stories in match-stick men, and then we will walk back to the railway station, wait for the train, and I will keep on drawing on the train. If the train trip is longer than an hour, I will set times for drawing and times for just looking out of the window. I have to say I get exhausted by drawing all these stories, because the same story gets repeated over and over again, but with different characters. Some of the stories are long and some are short. When I get tired, I tell William that I will draw three long stories and then only short ones, or very short ones. He can produce different length stories!

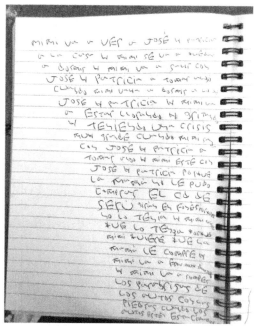

Photo of William's writing on his copybook. he always writes

in this increasingly angular way!

For Christmas 2011, William was invited to one of the other resident's house, but not long after arriving, he went into one of the bedrooms, got a pair of scissors and cut his fingers in several places, not badly enough to have stitches, only a plaster was required. That was the end of the party and he went home with his carer. Obviously, he was upset at not being able to be with me at Christmas. It was a tough time for me, but I could not be in two places at the same time!

William's (aged 33) review, written by the carers and home manager, for 2012 said:

- William's father died of cancer a few years ago, his brother, and then his mother moved to Argentina, and the friend who supported him on his trip to Argentina, and also invited him over to her house from time to time, moved to Australia. It appears that William has experienced a series of "significant" losses in his life. At times William gets extremely agitated and has prn medication to support him at these times. *I can imagine how sad all this was for William, and how difficult must be not to be able to express it in words, not to be able to tell a friend how he felt.*

- Many of the events previously described that have led to losses have "happened to William" and he has no control over them. It may benefit him to identify and agree with specific aspects of his life where he can genuinely be in control of making decisions for himself and feel that he is making choices rather than other people making them for him. Many people who have limited choice will react by pushing the boundaries and attempting to assert themselves, often in an inappropriate and potentially risky way. Staff can identify and agree with William areas in his life where he can take control safely.

- To support the development of positive self-esteem, an "Achievement Diary" could be created. The purpose of this is for William to reflect on and record his personal achievements. Achievements could range from doing his laundry, attending college, going shopping, helping someone, personal care, etc, etc. The aim is for the staff to give William positive feedback, and to redirect William to positive experiences if he is feeling negative about himself. a book of things he can be proud of! Staff reports that William likes to receive praise. *This was a very positive move that really helped William.*

- William can engage in lengthy periods of repetitive questioning and will continue until staff intervene. This is not easily done; William doesn't like to be redirected to another topic of conversation. A book of "Questions and answers" has been useful for this purpose. William can write his question and the staff will write the reply when William keeps repeating the same question he gets directed to his book.

- Routine, predictability, and sameness, are essential for William to feel safe. Consistently supporting William is important to avoid confusing or mixed messages. *I must emphasise this, consistency and avoiding mixed messages. This makes autistic children feel safe knowing that the message they receive is clear.*

- Effective communication is very important to William. William understands language in a literal way. By saying "pull your socks up" we mean "try harder", but to William, it means to pull his socks up. Staff need to ensure their language does not contain confusing statements and questions. Only one person should engage in conversation with him at a time.

- William appears to struggle to know how to start a conversation with people. William uses inappropriate comments when he wants to talk to somebody.

- Staff have identified that William has no social contact outside Rose House. Other residents have their families, and William sees this. The suggestion is a befriender scheme.

- Involve William in his Care plan by helping him to identify: What is important to me in my daily routine, what would I need to feel happy, what would I like doing, what new activity would I like to try.

- When offered a choice, William will answer open questions by saying "I don't know". It is better to say, for example, shall we go for a walk in Brockenhurst or Wilderley Wood?

- William may benefit from specially written social stories to describe a situation, concept or social skill. (Please see Carol Grey and social stories at www.thegraycenter.org) *Social stories, writing down, or drawing an explanation has always helped William to understand the message.*
- William can maintain some level of eye contact, dependent upon levels of mood and anxiety levels.
- When William is very anxious, he tends to stammer.

I'm mentioning William's reviews as I think they present a helpful way of describing his behaviour, and the attempts at solving his many issues.

I must comment on some of these points. Consistently supporting William has been very important, but it was not easy while I lived in Argentina. If William was anxious about something, he would phone me at any time of the day for me to give him the answer he was looking for. Most of the time, William would phone me before the staff had had time to contact me to agree on a course of action. William would phone me giving me his version of the problem, demanding an answer, and of course, my answer might not have been the same as the staff's answers, and this would cause him even more anxiety.

One of these controversial points was about dying and being born again. The manager of Rose House thought that it was wrong to let William believe that he was going to be born again. My belief was, and is, that nobody knows what happens after we die. If William wants to believe he is going to be born again, and it is his own way of sorting out his fear of dying, then why not? The manager persisted on this, and she was telling William that nobody knew what happened after one passed away. For the sake of consistency, I told William that I had been talking to some people from the church, and also that I had read an article in the paper stating that once we die nothing happens and the body becomes rigid, in the same way, a table is rigid and not alive. I even wrote something about it, making it look as though it had been copied from the newspaper. William didn't say anything then. The next time I went to visit him, he had gathered a lot of information to prove me wrong. One was a song, by an Argentine singer, that said, "so many times I have died and I'm still here". There was another song that said, "you have given me back my life". As usual, William was taking this literally, and could not understand the metaphorical meaning of these songs. Another evidence he had found in one of his books, stated that Hindus believe that to continue with the cycle of death and rebirth they need to bathe in the river Ganges! Well, this was the cherry on the pie! How could I argue with this reasoning? So, from then on, we continued talking about death and rebirth, and that was the end of the argument.

In June 2014, as usual, we booked into the Edinburgh Marriott Hotel. We arrived at Waverley Station, crossed the road, and took the airport bus to get off at the hotel. Not long after getting on the bus William started to ring the bell, to the annoyance of the bus driver. I was trying to pull his hand off the bell, but William is very strong, and he kept doing it. At one stage I got up and pretended that I was going to get off the bus and walk all the way to the hotel, and that seemed to do the trick and he stopped. Many times, when we have been on a bus, he pretends he is going to ring the bell, but he doesn't actually do it. He did not behave very well during our stay. He did not want to go to the pool or jacuzzi and went up and down the stairs too many times for my liking. The main problem was that sometimes he would go into another room if the door was open, and once he ended up in the basement and walked into the laundry room, almost running in, and frightened the staff. William was a man (age 35), not a little child, and to run into the laundry room was not very appropriate. When I explained to him that he had frightened the staff, he said: but it was just me, William. Autistic people, including William, think from their perspective outwards, reaching only one truth or logic, their own. So, why would the staff be frightened by him, he is harmless. William doesn't understand why people can't instantly understand his logic.

We stayed two nights at the hotel, and then took the train back home, a long journey of 7 hours. We had to change at Southampton Station. We'd had some delays, the train was very full, and we were tired. It was the rush hour, and I could see that many people had had a long day at work. We went to the exit five minutes before reaching the station. All of a sudden, William reached out and pulled the emergency stop lever. Our train stopped, plus all the associated trains in the same circuit. The guard came over, I explained to him about William's condition, and he was very understanding and did not charge us the hefty fine for

229

pulling the lever. I could hear people's annoyance, some of them had missed their connections, and they were not pleased. William understood and has never done it again. I also learnt from that experience, and we get up at the last minute when the train is already at the station, or I stand in front of William so he cannot get past to reach the lever.

William cannot feel empathy. If I tell him I've got a headache and cannot go to see him, his reaction will be: but I want you to get better and come, take some medicine and come.

Having said that, he is worried about one of the young men who lives with him and cannot talk. He told me he would like Tom (I have changed his name) to have brain surgery so he can speak again.

William continued breaking things, mostly his IT equipment. He also started to swallow things, like batteries, plastic objects, and even a small flash drive (memory pen/pen-drive) that I had sent him with music. Every time he swallowed something, he was taken to the hospital for an Xray and, fortunately, there were never any adverse consequences. This behaviour caused me a lot of anxiety and worries. His self-harming was becoming more serious.

Nigel and I were thinking of coming back to England for good. Although Nigel was very happy in Argentina, he was no longer breeding so many butterflies and he was thinking that maybe the time was right to come back home. We put our property for sale, but it was a big property, and the economy of the country was in dire straits.

William continued with his self-harming and started biting his tongue but much worse than before. On one occasion he bit it really hard, and with his fingernails pulled the split apart. It was stitched at the hospital and once at home, he pulled the stitches out. Once more he was taken to the hospital to be re-stitched, and once more he pulled the stitches out. In the end, his tongue was left to heal naturally.

Some years ago, I had the chance to talk to a teenager who was into self-harming. Layla was cutting her arms and thighs with a razor, bad enough to bleed, but not enough to need stitches. Layla told me that when she had a meltdown and was very anxious, it became so overwhelming that the only way to release tension was to self-harm. It was her only way to calm down again. I can only guess that William goes through the same process. Once self-harmed, or broke something, he regretted it and said sorry, promising he would never do it again, but he couldn't help himself.

Could it be that it is all related to communication issues? Could the key to stop self-harming be a better communication? If William was able to tell us exactly what is wrong with him maybe he would get rid of the awful anxiety that takes him to the extreme of self-harming. Would he feel calmer if he could communicate with the outside world, and with members of the community?

His carers had reported that William didn't know how to start a conversation, and sometimes he would swear to call attention. William had a Social Story that gave him instructions on the best way to speak to people if he wished to do so. Apparently, he was beginning to show some improvement in this area.

By now William was on some strong medication to try to calm him down. He was put on Citalopram, and Olanzapine, plus Lorazepan as PRN (Pro Re Nata: as needed). It didn't make me very happy to know he was on such strong medication, but I knew it was necessary and, right then, the only solution. It was not just a decision of his

GP, but a team of professionals were working towards helping William, and the medication was going to be reviewed regularly.

William self-harmed again shortly before Xmas, when he realised he was the only one to stay at home, and the other boys had gone to their parents' houses. This made me feel very guilty, and sad for him, but there was nothing I could do to sort it out at the moment.

I have just finished reading Temple Grandin's book: The Autistic Brain, and I would like to add some information from the book here.

Temple Gradin speaks about sensory over responsiveness and sensory under responsiveness, and I'm adding here my own comments after reading the book.

Sensory over responsiveness is when there is an overload of sensations, either visual, auditory or tactile. Some people with autism are overly sensitive to auditory input, they cannot stand loud noises, or when people speak, they hear a jumble of noises that they cannot process. Sometimes they feel like they are inside a loudspeaker at a concert.

I think William has tactile sensitivity as he doesn't like being touched. Some autistic people with bad tactile sensitivity feel pain when being touched.

Sensory under responsiveness is when there is poor or no response. This is the typical person with autism that doesn't respond when spoken to although there is nothing wrong with his hearing. William can sometimes be under-responsive if he chooses not to answer if spoken to. He is also under-responsive to pain, and I have given some examples through the book, but here is another one. One evening he was in his room, he wanted to get something from the long drawer at the bottom of his wardrobe, and the drawer came out completely and fell on his toes. He went to bed, and the following morning the carers found blood on his bedsheets, inspected his feet and saw where the drawer had grazed his toes and produced a big bruise. But William didn't say anything at all.

William stopped attending college courses. This was his choice as he was finding it quite a challenge to remain focused during the lessons.

His review stated that the best ways to support William through his anxiety incidents were:

- To remain calm, talk to him in a firm but affectionate way.

- To redirect him to go and listen to music until he calms down.

- To ask him to lie down, place his hand on his stomach and breathe deeply while slowly counting to 20.

- To suggest to him to go to his room to calm down, and after half an hour, if he is calm, try to debrief him.

- Reward charts. It can be divided in a.m and p.m, and William puts a tick in the appropriate box. At the end of the day, if he has two ticks, he gets a token to put into a jar. When he has seven tokens, he can exchange them for a reward of his choice, i.e., a train trip, a meal at a restaurant, etc.

In all the yearly reviews, the same challenging issue kept coming up:

William continues to have issues about his mum living in Argentina.

You can imagine how this made me feel! It was my fault that William was self-harming and feeling so low. I was very unhappy and desperate to go back to the UK, but we couldn't just pack up and return, we needed to sort out our issues as well before we could make the move. We were committed to returning as soon as we could sell our property.

Chapter Seven

Back to the UK for good

My father passed away in November 2017, and I felt I could come back to England without the guilt of not being with him at the end of his life.

Finally, in February 2018 we sold our property. We decided not to bring back a container, and we only packed personal things and books. We decided to downsize completely and bought a ground floor retirement flat in New Milton. Although it is a flat, it is in a complex of Maisonnettes, and ours is on the ground floor with a back door to the garden. It feels more like a house than like a flat. Our entire flat would fit into our former double garage and workshop in Rio Ceballos. We are half a mile from William's place, and this allows me to see him quite often.

Going back to when we just sold the house, as you can well imagine, there were a lot of things to sort out, money to be transferred internationally, a small removal to be organised, services to be cancelled, etc, etc. Fortunately, the new owners suggested that we could stay there, for as long as we needed to sort things out, in exchange for teaching them all about the maintenance of the property. There was the swimming pool, automatic watering, four different buildings, lots of plants in the garden and how to look after them, etc, etc. We became good friends, and we are still in contact.

William (aged 39) wanted me to give him the exact date of when I was going to arrive in New Milton. We were not sure of the date of our trip, but we thought that by the end of March we would be able to fly back home. To give us enough time to arrive, look at different properties, buy a car, etc, I told William that we were arriving on April 25th. We actually arrived on March 21st. We had been looking at some properties in the Rightmove app, and we were going to have a look at those after our arrival. A friend picked us up from the airport, and while we were in the car, I saw a ground floor flat in a retirement complex. I knew the street and liked the location. On arrival in New Milton we stayed at a lodge in the B&B where I had been staying every single June when coming to visit William. The following day we contacted the estate agent and agreed to have a viewing at 11am that same morning. We went to a car dealer and bought a car, and then went straight to the flat. It was love at first sight. There were things to be done to it, a lot of renovation, but we liked the fact that it felt like a house, and it was not in a block of flats.

As everything had been organised so quickly, and there was nothing else we could do until we got the keys to the flat, I decided to go and see William. I asked his keyworker to let me know when they were coming back from their outing and I went and rang the bell. When William saw me there his eyes were wide with surprise. Remember, he does not like unplanned experiences and breaks in his routine. William told me to go away and to come back on April 25th! I just laughed! As usual, once the penny dropped, and he had processed his feelings, he called me and told me to go and see him.

William was so happy to have me back that he stopped breaking things, self-harming, and he always had a smile on his face. If I asked him why he was so happy, he would say it was because I was back. I kept asking him every time I went to see him, it just sounded good to me to know he was happy again.

Fortunately, he did not want to come to our flat, and he did not want me to go and visit him in his own house. The agreement was that I would pick him up and we would go out. I picked him up every Monday. Three Mondays in a row went to Costa Coffee in Lymington (not far from New Milton), I picked him up at 10am and we were back about twelve. On the fourth Monday, we go out on a train trip and spent the whole day together.

William, and I guess it is part of his autism, has what I call The NO Syndrome. If you tell him he can't do something, he will certainly go out of his way to do it. If the pavement is icy and you tell him not to walk too fast as he might slip and fall, that is enough to make sure he will run along to see what happens. I have to be very careful how I warn him of danger as it could backfire and trigger the opposite response. I guess he doesn't realise the consequences of his actions and he just wants to check the result for himself.

William is clever, and he knows perfectly well what is dangerous, and how to provoke a reaction in me or in his carers. As part of his provocative conduct, he started to misbehave at the railway station. He would go to the edge of the platform, with his feet half over the edge, and not respecting the rule of standing behind the yellow line. To begin with, I would react the way he wanted me to react, telling him to get away, that it was dangerous, etc, etc. Then I started to ignore him and not even look at him, always fearing that he could fall down onto the rails. I am pretty sure that William will be very careful, and he knows the limits, but the fear is there anyway. Sometimes we stay in the waiting room of the railway station until the train comes, but he then finds something else to touch. One day we were on the platform waiting for the train, and there was another couple waiting as well. William was at the edge of the platform, looking back at me and waiting for my reaction. I ignored him, looking at my mobile phone but watching him from the corner of my eye. I could hear the couple talking about William, and the guy asked me if William was going to jump onto the rails. I told him I was hoping he would not do it, to which he replied: "So do we as otherwise we would be delayed!" I found his reply sad and I wondered if this is what everybody thinks when there has been a fatality, and there is an announcement that the service will be delayed because somebody has jumped or fallen onto the rails.

William pushes the limits of his trials; he would have made a good researcher!

William has a fascination with electricity, and he has a compulsion to touch all the cables, switches, sockets, etc that he finds as we walk along, or in the shops we visit. He also likes to touch the flaps that cover things like alarms, or fire buttons, and some letterboxes. I took him to Butlins for two nights. We arrived in the early afternoon, we went to the water park and he enjoyed all the water slides. The following day he went into an office, found a telephone and kept disconnecting it until I was contacted by the lifeguard. I thought he was going up and down the slides, but he was playing with the phone. Then he found a socket and he kept lifting the lid and touching it with his wet fingers. I was not worried as it was unlikely that he could get a shock, but the young lifeguard was very scared that he could get electrocuted. I had to take William away and went back to our room.

Touching cables in an electric box in Malaga, and on the street

In June we went to the Marriott Hotel in Edinburgh, and William behaved really well. Since he was a child, William has seen patterns on the pavements, not all the time, but sometimes he would stop, go back, have a look, jump over something that I couldn't see, and continue walking. This time, in Edinburgh, he saw these patterns with more frequency. He also started to jump on the metal covers on the pavements, the ones covering drains, gas, electricity, etc. He would jump on top to see if they would bend, collapse, or break. This was odd, and people would stop to look at him. William is a tall (1.88mtrs) and strong lad, and it was weird to see him jumping on the pavement.

He continues with this behaviour every so often. As we walked along the pavement, he kept looking for things to touch: the electricity boxes on the wall (they are closed and secure in this country), a shop-board on the pavement, sometimes he would ring the bell in a shop. He doesn't display this behaviour all the time, but when he has some anxiety it gets worse.

◇◇◇

In July 2018, Roderick, Zenny, and Jeremy came to the UK for a visit. I had told William about their visit and we talked about this in length. William said he did not want to see him, and he would see Roderick when he went to Argentina in 2020. Why, only William knew! He phones Roderick every Monday and sends him an email every week, so obviously there is some affection there. When Roderick and family came over, they arranged to pick William up one evening at 7pm to go to a pub. They arrived at 6.50pm, and William told them to wait until seven and went back to his room. They went to the pub, and Roderick bought William a big glass of coke, which he drank in one go, and then told him he wanted to go back home. Roderick convinced him to stay a bit longer, bought him another coke, took some selfies, and then took him back. I think they were in the pub for not longer than half an hour.

At the front: Zeni and William.

At the back: Jeremy and Roderick

I was trying to make up for all the years I had not been able to take him away more than once a year.

At the beginning of September, I went with William to Weymouth, and we stayed in an Airbnb flat. We stayed for three nights and William was very happy.

In February we went to Mallorca for a week with an all-inclusive trip. The hotel was great, with all the rooms surrounding a huge swimming pool. There was also a small water park but William was not interested at all. There were three restaurants, one serving fast food, one with an international buffet, and an Italian one. As William is such a fan of pasta, I thought he would be wanting to eat every meal at the Italian Restaurant, but he didn't want to go there at all, and we ate all our meals at the international restaurant.

The swimming pool was a great attraction, but sometimes he had difficulty finding our chairs if I was not there. This did not surprise me too much as all the loungers and all the towels were the same, the only difference was our bag and shoes left by the loungers.

There was a thatched bar by the pool, and the music equipment was on the counter. William could not help it and every so often he would go and disconnect it. The barman was very patient with him and didn't seem to mind. William liked sitting on the chairs by the bar to listen to the music. One day I could not see him in the pool, nor at the bar. There was a raised well where the water was pumped into the pool, and it was covered by a metal lid. William was jumping on this lid, and a big audience of kids and adults were watching him. I wonder what these people made of William. All in all, the trip went well, with minor odd behaviours, but nothing major.

For Christmas Eve, Christmas Day, and New-Years day, I took William out for the day and he was very happy.

In March 2019 I went to Argentina for a month, and I showed William my electronic ticket to reassure him that I was just going for a visit and I was definitely coming back. I had offered to take him with me, but he said he wanted to go to Argentina in 2020. Why in 2020 and not in 2019? Only William knows the answer.

William continues to talk about dying in two years-time, and changing the date as the new year approaches, now it is in 2023. But he has added something to his rebirth. Remember Marisa, his former teacher whom I virtually killed in a coach accident? Well, William wants her to be his mother when he gets born again! When I ask him what about me, his answer is "next time"! This amuses me greatly, and I would like to be able to understand his concept of "mother". Obviously, he feels great affection for Marisa.

Another of William's stories is when John Lennon was killed. He has made it up and it goes like this, I quote:

John Lennon was killed by a very bad man. When this bad man shot J.L, somebody saw him and called the police. When the police arrived and told the bad man that he was going to arrest him, the bad man cried because he didn't want to go to jail, but the policeman told him he was going to jail anyway and would remain there for 10 years. For the first two years of his jail sentence, the bad man was only allowed to eat hard bread and water, and to sleep on the floor. After two years he was given soup, and after four years he was also given pasta.

Another story that amuses William is something he watched on TV, in a program about airports, and which, of course, includes a bit of drama:

This lady takes a taxi to go to the airport, traffic is very heavy, and she can see she will be late. She arrives at the check-in desk but is told the gate has closed and she won't be able to board the plane. The lady starts to cry and begs the assistant to let her take the flight, to no avail, and she is told she should have left earlier to take into account the heavy traffic. And this is the bit William finds extremely funny.

Wherever we go, William likes to look at the buildings, chooses a tall one and makes out a story about "the dog" and one of his favourite characters. The dog would jump from the building when he goes there, but nobody sees it, and whoever has gone with the dog starts to look for him and enquires to see if somebody has seen him. Finally, he/she finds the dog on the pavement and calls the Vet. The Vet takes the dog to the Pet's Hospital and the dog remains there for a year until he recovers. The dog is taken to the airport, and he flies back to Argentina where the owner is waiting for him and tells him he has been a very silly dog, and he has missed him a lot.

Now the story takes a more dramatic twist as the dog goes to New York with Pochi Guell (our friend from Villa Silvina). Pochi is talking to a friend on the corner of the Empire State Building, the dog quietly walks away and climbs the stairs to the 102nd floor and jumps from a window. Obviously, the dog gets flattened on landing! Pochi starts looking for the dog and somebody tells her he had seen a dog jump from the top of the ESB. Pochi and her friend find the remains of the dog, they collect all the dog's body parts into a bag, they take a taxi and go to the cemetery to bury the dog. Pochi phones the owner in Salsipuedes, and when she tells him the sad news the owner starts to cry.

◇◇◇

I decided to spend Christmas with William, and I asked where he would like to go. William chose to go to

Lymington, about 3 miles from where we live. We rented a lovely flat in town for three nights. We went out to eat, for long walks, and spent some time in the flat drawing his stories. Again, all in all, he behaved well. He touched all the cables he could find in the flat and along the pavement, but that is William and he cannot help it.

William decided he would rather go to Malaga, Spain, than to Argentina. Why the change, only William knows and he did not want to tell me why, but it really suited me as I was dreading the long flight and the stay in Argentina. I was afraid that William would insist on visiting all his former teachers and people in Salsipuedes, but those people might not want to invite William over as he is not a child any longer, but a big 42-year-old man.

William wanted to go to a self-catering bungalow, but I explained to him that if he wanted to be in Malaga town, it could either be a flat, or an all-inclusive holiday like the one we had in Mallorca. Finally, he agreed on a flat, and I booked one through Airbnb, in the centre, close to the beach and to all the facilities. We flew to Malaga on Feb 4th, 2020 and came back on the 12th.

William always sits on the back seat in the car, and I always put on the child-lock to prevent him from opening the door when the car is moving. We took a taxi from the airport to the flat, about 30-minutes' drive. I asked the taxi driver to put the child-lock on, but apparently it is against the law to do so in case there is an accident or a fire….and it makes sense. William was opening and closing the door the whole time, and we had to stop three times to close it properly. We arrived at the flat, left our things, and went to Carrefour Express, just round the corner, to buy a few things as it was late afternoon. While I was doing the shopping, William found a drawer with croissants that were being kept hot, and decided to open it and close it all the time, I think he aimed to see if it would fall. I think he was anxious about not having the child-lock on in the taxi. It seems contradictory that he would open and close the door but wanted the child-lock on. The fact that he cannot open the door, and that the temptation to open it cannot be satisfied, gives him some kind of security.

Many times, when William is in "breaking mode", he tells me he wants to go and stay in a castle until he learns how to stop breaking things. Or he wants me to remove the item of his fixation.

We had spent all day travelling and we were tired, so it was an early night for us. The following day we went out for a long walk, went up to the Alcazaba, the Moorish castle, and looked around the cathedral and other old buildings. William wanted to buy a CD of an Argentine singer, thinking that they might have it in Spain, but the shop assistant had never heard of this singer, and William felt frustrated.

Our flat was on the fourth floor and had a small patio with a protected wall of about 1.50mtrs overlooking the ground floor flat patio. William was trying to climb the wall and started to make out a story about the dog jumping from the wall to the patio on the ground floor.

I'm still not sure why he became so anxious, but he was trying to break everything in the flat. He was pulling the tube of the intercom and would then let go. Finally, I disconnected it and hid it. Then he was tipping the tall wine glasses, again I had to hide them. He went for the bedside table lamps, nice and tall ceramic ones. Those were hidden as well.

One evening he had a terrible meltdown, shouting as if I was torturing him. He went on and on and I could not calm him down. Fortunately, nobody knocked on our door or called the police. I was very scared that if the police came William could be sectioned as he was out of control. The following day William told me he was annoyed because the clock was going to change in October, and he didn't want that to happen. That was the reason he gave to his carers when we came back. William was fine when we were out walking, and oh boy we did some walking! We got up late, had a shower, breakfast, and out we went. We walked mostly along the beach, stopping every so often to sit on a bench and have a drawing session. We came back to the flat in the evening, had dinner, and went to bed. Everything had been hidden, and if William had searched, he would have found the hidden items, but it seemed that out of sight out of mind. He always found something to touch, and fortunately, he never saw the Fuse Box.

One evening, as usual, the subject of death came up. William started to ask me about heart attacks, and how soon somebody who's had a heart attack would die. I could not explain to him that it depended on the circumstances, how bad it was, etc, etc. It had to be a black and white explanation. I told William that a person having a heart attack would die after two hours if he had not been taken into hospital, or contacted the doctor for some medication. His answer was: "But Grandad had his heart attack during the night, and he was taken into hospital in the afternoon, but he didn't die." And he was right! He had been on the ball all the time, appeared to be oblivious, but he was sucking in every single detail….and storing it in his memory. And he has shown this behaviour many times.

We went back to the airport with the same taxi driver, and William opening the door! The flight back was all right, then we took the train, and arrived in New Milton at midnight.

This trip opened my eyes to what could have happened, it could have been worse, and I was completely on my own in a foreign country. He could have been sectioned, I could have been accused of torturing or abusing him and taken into custody. We both speak Spanish, but that is not the case. So, I decided that from then on, I would only take him away within the UK.

A week after coming back from Malaga, I went to Argentina for a visit. I talked to William and he told me that I had to go every year to Argentina for a visit, but I was not going to go there to live ever again, and I gave him that reassurance.

I left the UK on Feb 21st, 2020 and was due to return on March 25th,2020, but due to Corona Virus Argentina decided to close its frontiers, cancelled all flights from the 17th, and I had to book an earlier flight on the 15th. I arrived and we have been in lockdown since then. I could not see William, and this made him very anxious. He started displaying some self-harming behaviour again. William wanted maintenance to come and remove the fire door device that makes the door close slowly by itself. He wanted this done because he wanted to be able to slam the door on his tongue. He was putting his tongue between the door and the door frame and closing it, but nothing happened.

Only at the end of April, when the government allowed us to meet one person from another household, I was able to see William again.

When I told him I could go and pick him up, and go out together, he said he did not want to see me until the end of Covid19. William had to process this in his own time. After a few days, he told me he was happy to go out with me again.

This calmed him down, and since then, he has been happy and far more relaxed. He also accepted to go out for walks and picnics with Sarah, his keyworker. Fortunately, the weather has been amazing since the beginning of April, and William has been to the beach several times for a picnic and was happy to sit there and chill out. I have been taking him out, on Saturdays and Sundays, for a walk to a local lake. There are picnic tables there where we can sit, and I can draw his stories.

When we go out, William always takes two atlases: one of Argentina, and a world atlas, plus three copybooks. Last weekend he told me that he had put one of the pages of his black copybook against the light bulb in the Quiet room, and the corners were brown where they were slightly burnt. We discussed the heat of the lamp, that it could catch fire, and the danger of the fire spreading. William kept saying that if it caught fire, he was going to put it out with a glass

256

of water. I kept saying he wouldn't be able to put it out with just a glass of water, and the conversation went on and on until I took him back home. The following day, as soon as we went out, he resumed the conversation, and I decided to change strategy, and this has worked out many times when William is in a contradictory mood. I just said to him: "William, you are a very clever man, you know very well what you can do and what is dangerous, so I won't tell you what to do. You are very intelligent, it is your house, and your copybook, and it is not for me to tell you what to do." End of discussion. William could push the limits and go to the edge of a dangerous action, but he is not stupid and won't go any further. It has always worked to encourage what he can do!

As he has been behaving extremely well since I started taking him out again, I decided to order a calendar, and a set of 180 Happy Faces Stickers. William was very pleased with this, and he has been sticking a happy face on the calendar most nights. Some nights he has told me he has not done it because he has not "been perfect", either swearing or provoking Mathew (one of the other residents). It breaks my heart to think he is so honest! When he has not been good, he writes sad face on the calendar for that day!

I mentioned before that William sends me three emails a day, and each email is addressed to: Dear Grace, and signed: William Elliott.

Examples of some of his emails:

Jeremy is having breakfast like Chubby Lomond.

I have to answer: Nooo, like Chubby Checker, and like Loch Lomond.

And there are many combinations of names, like Patti Waverly (Nooo, like Patti Labelle and like Edinburgh Waverley Station), etc, etc.

When it is night-time in the North Pole it is also night-time in the South Pole.

My answer: No, impossible as they are in different hemispheres. Again, there are variations of the same subject.

William likes to send me the timeanddate.com website of different cities, especially those in the far north, in Iceland, Scandinavia, or far South like Usuahia. He likes to check the length of the days in these cities during the year. In my answers I have to tell him how long is the day in that particular city, or that there is daylight all day long, or that it is dark all day long.

Some mails are about his longer stories and require some specific answers.

He also sends emails to my cousins Annie and Marina, to my sister, to Analia (Roderick's former wife), and to Gaby (who took him to Argentina in 2008). Because his mails could be quite long, and they require a specific answer, I have agreed with all these friends to forward William's emails to me, I answer them and send them back to the recipient, then they just have to copy and paste and send them to William as their own answer.

I have also mentioned that William had difficulty concentrating and focusing on his classes at the local college. The main problem, and this is applicable to many persons with autism, is that a minor detail can catch their attention, and this will prevent them from focusing again on what is required. William told me that the teacher had a jacket with different colour buttons, and he was watching those buttons and could not follow what she was saying. I remember a story of an autistic person that loved to watch

The Flintstones, but he couldn't follow what was going on because he loved to watch their feet, and nothing else.

◇◇◇

Before, I mentioned that my cousins call me "The Phantom Killer", and that I have, in my imagination, killed Marisa (William's former teacher), and the poor guy who went to buy the bricks to build the runway by Granja Pia. Those were just two of my many "phantom victims", and this is why I chose the title for this book.

In 2007, William told me that he wanted the TV producers to put some of his stories in a TV program. The main characters were the three guys he liked most at Granja Pia. Of course, the problem was that these stories had not been previously filmed, and they were only in William's imagination. I tried to explain to him that this was not possible, but he wanted to know why it was not possible. I tried the best I could and, finally, I just said that the technology to do so had not been invented yet. And this was my downfall! I've dug myself into a hole! William got hooked on this and told me that it was very simple, just look for an inventor to invent this technology! And so I did and obviously, I found an imaginary inventor. And the story unfolded from then on. This inventor had to look for special materials and tools to invent this very difficult technology....and took several months to find everything he needed. I had to "phone" him every so often to get an update of his progress. And when he was very close to having the technology ready, this inventor got cancer and died. (another one of my phantom victims).

I had to then start looking for another inventor, and finally, I found one. Of course, he had to start from scratch, but once he had almost done it, the gas cylinder in his workshop exploded and the poor inventor died, and everything in his workshop got destroyed. (yet another one of my phantom victims).

Again, I had to look for another inventor who started from scratch, same old chestnut, and this poor guy got attacked in a dark street and killed. (One more to add to my reputation).

Once more I found another inventor willing to give it a try. I told William it was difficult finding one as it had become a dangerous profession!

And like that the story continued and the years went past, until last year that I decided to have some DVDs made, in Argentina, with two of his stories. A friend of mine, in Rio Ceballos, who is a brilliant video producer, did a fantastic job. It was not exactly what William expected because he wanted his friends to actually appear in the film. I told him this was what could be done right then, but William is very persistent, and he asked me to go back to the inventor to beg him to start working straight away to improve the technology. So, I "phoned" the inventor who told me that for a whole year he had to work at a factory and could not dedicate any more time at the technology until November 2020 when he was retiring. All this was just to gain time and see what excuse I could find then. It is now May 2020, and the Coronavirus has killed many people. This is the perfect excuse; my inventor will soon be dying of Covid19. Poor guy, he is another one of my phantom victims. I know that when I tell William, in October, I will be on my way to look for another inventor, but time goes by and the story will keep unfolding. I think William knows it is a kind of game, and we both enjoy it.

William is now 41 years old!

Epilogue

Nigel and I, 2019

To finish this story, I would like to say that William is like
the boy in this poem:

There was a little boy,

who had a little curl in the middle of his forehead,

and when he was good, he was very very good,

but when he was bad, he was horrid!

His behaviour, sweet or horrid, is the same as his likes or dislikes, everything is black or white, no grey areas!

I either want to hug him and kiss him, which I can never do because he doesn't like to be touched, or I want to literally kill him!

When William is going through a period when he is calm and has no major anxieties, he is as happy as Larry and he enjoys life to the full, laughing and smiling all the time. When something is causing him anxiety, he is miserable and he is difficult to cope with.

I must confess that there have been times when I had harboured the idea of abandoning William, promising to close my heart and not care what happens to him from that point on. Of course, these horrible feelings don't last for more than half an hour, and then I feel guilty for thinking something so very selfish! I'm writing this for the benefit of any parent of an autistic person, only she, or he, will be able to understand how I feel at times.

Having a son with autism is like being in a roller coaster, there are ups and downs, with speedy bits, you want to scream with fear and overwhelming feelings, and you love and enjoy all the bits in between. It educates you;

it makes you creative; you become a researcher, and you stretch your brain trying to work out what is the best way to approach different situations. You become embarrassed when you are in a public place and your child displays weird behaviour, and then you learn to build a shield, like a thick skin around you so these situations stop hurting you.

You have a love-hate relationship, but as a mother/father you will always love them dearly, no matter what! As I have mentioned before, I am lucky as William is now in a safe environment, in a lovely house, and very well looked after by Dimensions-uk.org, accredited by Social Services. In spite of knowing that William will always be safe and looked after, I can't help but worry about how he would cope once I'm not in this world any longer. It breaks my heart to think that he will be on his own, as Roderick (his brother) lives in Argentina, and if he comes to see William it would only be for a short visit. I have enjoyed my life so far, and I wouldn't change any part of it. I have no regrets. Of course, I would have liked William to be "normal", for his sake not for mine. I love William as he is. He has taught me to be patient, and to see what is important in life. It has not been easy, but I have learnt to deal with it the best I could. Many well-intentioned friends, and relatives, have told me that I have given William my best, that he is an adult now, that he has his own life, and I should let go a bit. But I am the mother of a person whose brain is wired in a different way, and this makes him a very special person, so special that this makes me go to him with all my heart.

I must say that having a son with autism, or special needs, or drug addiction, etc, is not easy. If you are married, or in a relationship, unless you both agree on how to approach everything, pulling forward together, there is no chance of staying together for long. It is just too devastating, and it kills the relationship.

Something that has always helped me has been to look around. There is always somebody worse off than you. I'm lucky that William has classic autism, and not a physical disability as well.

I have never been to a therapist for support or help, when I feel down, I talk to Nigel, or to my friends (I include here my cousins who are my friends as well). Going for a walk also helps to blow the cobwebs away!

Life with William has been like a long road, coming to forks that made me choose one way or the other, sometimes I was right, and sometimes I had to go back to the fork to follow the other road.

Sometimes it ended in a maze where it appeared to be no way out, but after a while of going one way, turning back and choosing another way, William and I made it out of the maze. Sometimes it felt like being through a very dark tunnel, but at the very end there was always a light.

The poet Robert Frost, finishes *The Road Not Taken* with these words:

Two roads diverged in a wood, and I—
I took the one less travelled by,
And that has made all the difference.

Life is a journey, and decisions have to be made, which way should I go? It will make all the difference depending on the road you take.

With an autistic child, nobody can tell you exactly which road to take. They can tell you that this road has a better surface, or it is very bumpy, to take that other one with less traffic, or this one with terrific views. In the end, YOU, as a mother, will know which is the best road to make your life-journey with your son a happy one. You have to make your own path and walk it together.

Always remember that without challenges life could be far too boring. Having a son with autism will provide you with all the challenges you need to make your life a good adventure!

It is now June 2020, and my journey with William goes on.

William, Spring 2020

Printed in Great Britain
by Amazon